AFTER THE FALL

AFTER THE FALL

Resurrecting Your Life From Shame, Disgrace, and Guilt

Donald Hilliard, Jr.

Destiny Image® Publishers, Inc.
P.O. Box 310
Shippensburg, PA 17257-0310

"Speaking to the Purposes of God for this Generation
and for the Generations to Come."

For Worldwide Distribution, Printed in the U.S.A.

ISBN 10: 0-7684-2496-8

ISBN 13: 978-0-7684-2496-6

This book and all other Destiny Image, Revival Press, MercyPlace, Fresh Bread, Destiny Image Fiction, and Treasure House books are available at Christian bookstores and distributors worldwide.

For a U.S. bookstore nearest you, call
1-800-722-6774.

For more information on foreign distributors, call
717-532-3040.

Or reach us on the Internet:
www.destinyimage.com

1 2 3 4 5 6 7 8 9 10 11 / 09 08 07

Endorsements

With a sensitivity that is characteristic of Bishop Donald Hilliard, an uncomfortable issue and sin is exposed in his book, *After the Fall*. Rather than throw away those who have "fallen from grace," Bishop Hilliard shows the Church of the Redeemed how to reclaim them with the love and mercy of our Lord.

> —Cynthia L. Hale, D. Min.
> Senior Pastor
> Ray of Hope Christian Church

Bishop Donald Hilliard has written a much-needed book. In a "season" of litigation where a litigious public is focusing in on persons who have been abused sexually, even the Church of Jesus Christ seems to have forgotten about the abusers! Bishop Hilliard's book speaks to both the abused and the abuser.

Much ministry, much therapy, much counseling and much prayer are needed when sexual abuse has taken place in the religious community. Repentance and restoration are still the work of God and God's Church, however, and those are the issues that Bishop Hilliard's book addresses.

God is a God of restoration. Bishop Hilliard's work seeks to *restore* both the abused and the repentant abuser to community in the same loving way that Jesus Christ restored those who had sinned. I commend this book highly and recommend it to all who are serious about the ministry of reconciliation.

—Reverend Dr. Jeremiah A. Wright, Jr., D. Min.
Senior Pastor
Trinity United Church of Christ
Chicago, Illinois

This book will help us understand theologically how God is able to reach us at our lowest point, lift us up, and place us back where we belong. Bishop Hilliard has done a great service to the Christian community and specifically the African American community, by offering such a powerful book that provides not only intellectual depth but also theological reflection.

—Otis Moss, III, M. Div.
Pastor

When I began to read your introduction, I was again made to see what an awesome God we as the chosen and his disciples, serve. I was amazed to see that our hearts for preaching, teaching, and showing forgiveness are of the same mindset. As God should guide, my doctoral studies' thesis is founded on "Healing the Wounded Healer." I am convinced we all must recognize that in order to be forgiven, we must first be willing to forgive, thus the process of restoration, healing, and letting go of guilt and shame.

I heartily endorse your endeavor to publish your book, *After the Fall*, compelling the Church of the redeemed to extend to others mercy and grace such as God has given them over, and over, and over, and over.

—Reverend Jasmin 'Jazz' Sculark, M. Div.
God's Servant, Shiloh's Pastor

DEDICATION

This book is dedicated to the greater glory of God and to all who have a sincere desire, through it all, to finish strong.

TABLE OF CONTENTS

FOREWORD

THE greatest test of character is the ability to rise after a fall. Many leaders throughout history have successfully climbed the ladder of greatness, notoriety, fame and power only to fall at the mercy of some poor personal judgment, moral failure, or compromise in integrity. It seems that many use their gifts to make it to the top, but lack the character to maintain their achievements.

However, failing and falling is not the worst thing in life; but it is the ability and challenge of getting up again and rising from the ashes of despair. In most cases, many who fell did not succeed in their bid to emerge from their failure effectively, and there are many reasons for this. Some did not succeed because of their incorrect response to the process of corrections, others because of their lack of submission to leadership's authority, still others because of personal pride that produced a spirit of deception and delusion. Little has been written on the subject of restoring, rebuilding, and repairing a fallen soul. So this work is a welcomed addition to the process of salvaging those who fall.

Bishop Donald Hilliard, II in this work, *After the Fall*, addresses this issue of restoration after a fall and, in his unique way, presents principles that provide instructions, philosophy, and action steps we can take to help ourselves and others come back from a fall. He leaps over complicated theological jargon to present simple precepts so that all who desire to help others regain their balance and rebuild their character can apply them effectively.

I am deeply impressed with this work and hope it becomes a manual to help restore and salvage the valuable gifts and potential still trapped within those who have fallen and may fall. Read the wisdom on each page and embrace the healing power and grace of a second chance.

—Dr. Myles E. Munroe
Founder and President
BFM International
ITWLA
Nassau, Bahamas

FOREWORD

HOW does a parent arm a child to win a battle that he/she hasn't conquered, especially when incidents of moral failure have been normalized or dismissed? For sure, when the behavior of disgrace isn't owned as sin and discarded, restoration becomes a ship with neither wind nor water. Repentance and responsibility proceed restoration, and neither acknowledgement nor regret are repentance. "I'm sorry" isn't the same as "forgive me."

To see ourselves in the eyes of a "criminal" can stay the exercise of conscience, cause a landslide of condemnation, or enroll us in the aerobics of avoidance. Have we minimized offenses because we knew the offender had something on us? Yes. Have we condemned in others what we couldn't or wouldn't control in ourselves? Sometimes. Have we excused others because we needed their gifts? Probably. Individually and corporately, compromise can weaken the hands of good intention until they are unable to take hold of fallen destiny. Hence, retrieving integrity and a love where correction, compassion, and affirmation are interwoven is essential to facilitating "the comeback" of another.

The hope of restoration and the mystery of transformation intersect. Jesus probably didn't restore Lazarus to a diseased existence. He probably transformed the systems of his body and then restored him to life. Neither are we restored until transformation has happened. So we're left to wrestle with the ways of human nature, culture, the demonic, and the cross of Christ. Can the power of God permeate personality, chemistry, and moral choice? Absolutely. If not, the Bible is suspect, Jesus died in vain, and I am still lost! Read this book. Ponder its message. Initiate head and heart adjustments, and restore others once your footing is secure.

—The Reverent Bernadette Glover-Williams, D. Min.
Executive Pastor
Cathedral International
Perth Amboy, New Jersey

PREFACE

WEBSTER'S dictionary defines shame as "a painful feeling of guilt for improper behavior, etc.; dishonor or disgrace."

As we look at ourselves in the mirror today, we notice that there are far too many of us who possess unlimited potential, possibilities, and promise, but who will regrettably never come to know the fullness of our destiny because of shame. The power of shame is such that it locks us into a closet, even if the closet is within our own minds. We just can't seem to forget what occurred when we were children, when the marriage dissolved, and when our parents left home. We never seem to forget the marks of abuse that remain unseen, when we were molested, when we went bankrupt, and when our sin was uncovered.

We hide from the shame of being removed as a church leader. We hide from the hurtful effects we caused our loved ones when we chose our work over our commitment to loving our family. We stand tall in the public light, but we shamefully hide in darkness, knowing we haven't called our ailing mother or our homeless uncle. The world knows us as its movers and shakers, but our web browsers know us as slaves to pornography and sick, unspoken fetishes. Yes, we as leaders earn more, but we also hide more. It's true. We see more, but we also scheme more.

This series was preached at our church to reach for the backslidden believer and the fallen leader. *The Way Back From Shame* has become one of our best-selling series because it is a practical and descriptive manual designed to aid those who have fallen from the pinnacle of success. This book is based on that series.

After the Fall: Resurrecting Your Life From Shame, Disgrace, and Guilt represents the real heartbeat of my ministry. I believe that the grace and mercy of God can pull anyone out of shame, regardless of what the root cause of that shame may be.

For the rejected individual, whether Christian or non-Christian, this book offers explicit examples of how God restores a person to complete wholeness and recovery from shame. No matter your profession (prostitute, pastor, or CEO), God has a plan for your life. No matter your circumstance or experience (whether it be incest, rape, or divorce), God is still sovereign and desires to uplift and breathe life onto the broken, bruised, and bereaved. Rest assured in knowing that you are not alone.

King David was locked in shame because of his sin against God. Moses was hesitant to come forward to serve the Lord because he was locked in his own shame. Even the apostle Peter was locked in shame after denying the Lord. It was not until the Lord restored Peter that Peter walked into his purpose and destiny in God.

What message does this book aim to convey? The message is simple: *God is looking for you. It is time to come out of the closet and out of the back of the church. Come down from the ninth balcony and get your name, song, prayer life, and dignity back. The Lord is calling you by name—and your name is no longer shame. . . .*

The news is littered with various stories of leaders who have fallen. Corporate executives, politicians, and clergy have all fallen from their pedestals of influence. It is not my intention to make light of anyone's indiscretion or sin, yet I *do* want to let both the violated and the violator know that there is grace available for the wounded soul. Regardless of whatever, whomever, and whenever, the grace and mercy of God is strong enough to deliver all from the power and the clutches of shame. God's grace is available to all, and while there may not be a reinstatement to an office or position of power, there can be restitution and renewal in one's own heart and soul.

I encourage all of you not just to read through the pages of this, my latest work, but also, with bated breath, to pray for deliverance. Every page will cut deeper and deeper at the callus that has become the hiding place of your shame until you are free from its damning effects on your soul. The Truth *will* set you free!

ACKNOWLEDGEMENTS

I am extremely grateful for the many people who helped me with this project. This has indeed, been a tremendous journey for me, and I know that without the tremendous support from my editorial team and staff this book just would not have been completed.

I especially wish to thank the Reverend Larry Walker at Walker & Associates; the Reverend Christopher Michael Jones; Minister P. Simone Hankerson, my executive assistant and right arm; Deacon Sylvia Haire, my personal manager and other arm; Ms. Giavonnie Wallace; the entire Cathedral International Staff, for covering those who have fallen from grace and dignity; and Cathedral Productions, for your tireless service in duplicating my meager efforts at preaching. I am also deeply appreciative of all of those faithful sons and daughters in faith who took the time to read and evaluate the subject matter and manuscript.

Finally, I am grateful for my family:

—my mother, Alease Hilliard-Chapman, who after all these years still gets excited over my latest literary endeavor, as if it was my first one;

—my beloved wife of 24 years, Phyllis Denise;

—and my precious children, Leah Joy Alease, Charisma Joy Denise, and Destiny Joy Thomas.

Finally, to the One who sits high and looks low, whose Holy Spirit sustains my life and in whose name I am humbled to write, teach, and preach...even Jesus, the very Christ of God.

INTRODUCTION

T HE pain hit so close to home that it broke my heart. The shame that brought the pain came from the acts of one of my own staff ministers, from a friend and coworker in my church organization.

His acts would have been grounds for instant dismissal, defrocking, and public rebuke, and in many churches this man would have been openly shunned for life and given the "left foot of fellowship" without so much as a tear or a prayer. It often seems as if the family of God prefers to "shoot its wounded" and "tend to its offenses." This is especially common when a person's shame becomes a family's shame, or one's sins somehow besmirch the reputation of a church or religious community.

However, there is a better way. It has *nothing* to do with condoning wrong behavior or unwise decisions; nor does it require "loosening" Bible-based theology to overlook heresy or outright sin. Sin is sin. Sin is unacceptable to God, regardless of its kind, flavor, or degree. He warned us that *"without shedding of blood, there is no remission* [of sins]" (Heb. 9:22 NKJV). Therefore, God sent His Son to shed His innocent blood to wash away, remove, and utterly destroy all sin in our lives. We should continually thank Him for providing the ultimate cure for sin, for *each* of us must *constantly* draw on that inexhaustible account and divine prescription.

But how quickly we forget! The problem seems to be that we are quick to expect mercy and grace when the sin is ours, but just as quick to deliver condemnation and judgment when the sin is our neighbor's. (Of course, we would never actually *call* it "condemnation and judgment." We prefer kinder, gentler, and more religious terms such as "conviction and correction.")

This habit of dispensing human judgment rather than divine mercy produces a harvest of destruction, hypocrisy, and bitterness. This, in turn, yields what the Bible calls the "*desolations of many generations*" (Isa. 61:4).

Isaiah the prophet would recognize this judgmental attitude instantly and condemn it as disobedience. He prophesied under the influence of the Holy Spirit that the afflicted, the broken-hearted, the prisoners, and those in mourning who are transformed through Jesus Christ the Messiah would:

rebuild ancient ruins,

raise up former devastations,

repair ruined cities, and

[repair] the desolations of many generations (see Isa. 61:4).

In effect, we've managed to reverse the blessing to make it a curse. When someone among us falls or stumbles, we use our words, our political clout, our ecclesiastical position, or our old-fashioned gossip skills to afflict them, break their hearts, imprison them, and drive them into mourning.

We need to remember that the anointing demonstrated by Christ in the cross is able to *"break every yoke"* of bondage (Isa. 58:6). The passionate soul of this book is the living reality that *the cross and the blood triumph over every sin, as long as there is repentance.* There is a way back from shame! Now let us live, think, and minister in obedience to that eternal truth.

Read on if you dare. It is time for the Church of the Redeemed to extend to others as much mercy and grace as it has received! Amen.

Chapter 1

PARALYZED BY SHAME

Shame!

Carefully positioned cameras capture politicians, police captains, doctors, lawyers, billionaire chief financial officers, prostitutes, and child molesters *in the spotlight of shame*. Armies of professional and amateur camera men wait to capture them "in the act" by day and by night. Seeking escape from the shame, many of the accused desperately struggle to hide their identity or preserve some measure of their dignity: They raise shirts over their heads, coats over their faces, briefcases in front of cameras, and hands over bared body parts. They are caught, accused, and paraded in front of the public eye with no place to run.

Shame overtakes most of us far from the glaring lights of TV crews. Yet it always seems that just enough people—or even just the one *right person*—witness our descent into sin and error, or the horror of another person's abusive ways. Then shame roars in to paralyze us with fear and shock us with shame's consequences.

You would think Christians are "immune" to shame, but it isn't true. Although God can use shame to bring us to full restoration, He usually doesn't get the chance. We usually take the shame and run away from Him, unwilling to admit its source or accept His healing.

Far too many of us fail to come into our full destiny and apparently abort our future because we remain shrouded in *shame*. We feel sidelined, benched, or totally dropped from God's roll because we missed the mark. We lifted our hand from the plow of God in some way and totally missed His promised place.[1] We fear that our sins or shortcomings have forfeited the position that God had for us.

LIVES CONTORTED AND TWISTED BY UNRELENTING SHAME

Some of us, wounded by the betrayal of our friends or most trusted family members, struggle with lives that are contorted and twisted by unrelenting shame and dark sorrow. We watch helplessly as our once promising futures and bright hopes brutally disintegrate and self-destruct right before our eyes.

Anyone and everyone scarred by the affliction of shame knows what it feels like to cry out to the heavens. In the heart language of the weeping prophet, Jeremiah: "Is there no balm in Gilead? Can we find no comfort, solace, and hope in the God we serve?"

The harvest is past, the summer has ended and the gathering of fruit is over, yet we are not saved! [comes again the voice of the people.] For the hurt of the daughter of my people am I [Jeremiah] hurt; I go around mourning; dismay has taken hold on me. Is there no balm in Gilead? Is there no physician there? Why then is not the health of the daughter of my people restored? (Jeremiah 8:20-22 AMP)

The saddest part of this picture is that we usually lose our way over something that *God has already forgiven!* The power of the cross becomes obscured by the shadow of our crushing pain—whether we mourn over our sins and indiscretions or simply groan over wounds that God covered long ago under the blood. The power of pointing fingers and accusing lips was taken away long ago, but we continue to suffer in our cage of condemnation as if no one told us. We still live the life of the condemned, totally unaware of God's great gift to us!

MANY HAVE FALLEN FROM GRACE INTO THE CRUEL ARMS OF SHAME

Perhaps you or someone close to you is constantly tormented with the thought: "I made such a mess out of my life! Why would God continue to bother with me at all?" It's no wonder that so many people feel that way. Shame lurks at the doorway of our every sin, wrong motive, wrong decision, or betrayal. It also haunts the shadowy memories of every act of abuse or misuse perpetrated against us by others.

Shame has no power over us when we learn to live in grace, but most of us just aren't there yet—at least not all the time. And many have fallen from grace into the cruel arms of shame. Perhaps that explains why the word shame appears exactly 100 times in the King James Version of the Bible, with even more related words showing up from cover to cover![2] I've found no less than *20 different words* (12 in Hebrew and 8 in Greek) that were used by the inspired biblical writers to describe and illustrate the depth and sorrow of shame![3]

Our single English word, on the other hand, struggles to fully represent all the pain and damage inflicted by uncontrolled and unmanaged shame raging *apart from* God's grace. *Webster's Collegiate Dictionary* defines *shame* this way:

1a: a painful emotion caused by consciousness of guilt, shortcoming, or impropriety;

1b: the susceptibility to such emotion

2: a condition of humiliating disgrace or disrepute: ignominy

3a: something that brings censure or reproach; also: something to be regretted: PITY ("It's a shame you can't go")

3b: a cause of feeling shame.[4]

With all due respect to *Webster's*, defining *shame* this way is like defining cancer merely as "a disease." It is technically true but woefully inadequate. To understand the paralysis of shame, you have to *experience* it.

IT IS LIKE A DORMANT VIRUS OR DISEASE
WAITING FOR THE NEXT OPPORTUNITY

Unfortunately, most of us don't have to look very hard or very far to find shame. It makes its home in the carefully hidden rooms of our secret lives, waiting like some dormant virus or disease for the next opportunity to spring back onto center stage and dominate our lives. (Come to think about it, shame has some strong similarities to cancer!)

My heart especially goes out to the many who suffer the pain of shame *innocently*, as victims, through no fault of their own. It appears the majority of these victims are women or children. It also seems that the very men who should be their protectors, providers, equippers, and heroes in life most often inflict the pain behind their shame!

Perhaps you have been betrayed in a relationship. If so, then you could describe firsthand how it feels to be betrayed. You may know the sinking feeling that comes when you look into someone's eyes knowing that even though he or she says, "I'm sorry," you may never really know if you can trust them again—because they've lied. It is painful to discover the reality behind God's words of wisdom, "*The heart is deceitful above all things, and desperately wicked: who can know it?*" (Jer. 17:9).

Prepare yourself for a graphic, reality-based illustration of pure unrelenting shame. This is no shallow, plastic, dramatized reenactment of shame and sorrow or some sympathy play. This is the Bible at its brutally honest best, as it reveals the searing, unyielding, hope-consuming realm of unjustified, undeserved, and seemingly unconquerable shame!

In Hot Lust and
With Cold Malice...

Let me take you to one of the most frightening and troubling texts in the Bible. It is the true story of royalty, of a prominent prince who cruelly premeditates a crime of so-called passion against his royal half-sister. Both the victim and the victimizer were children of one of the most famous men in human and biblical history: King David.

Amnon, the malefactor in this story, cruelly executed his plan with the help of a shrewd and cold-hearted friend. In hot lust and with cold malice, he brutally *raped his own sister* and then threw her out in the street like a discarded rag with no fear of prosecution! (He knew his famous father was too weak-hearted to act against him.)

If the same crime happened *today*—even in our sex-jaded society where public tolerance of deviant lifestyles has become a national "virtue"—*this crime* would headline the evening news and dominate the tabloid sheets for months. The story would attract live, round-the-clock coverage from news organizations around the world. (And made-for-TV movies would be sure to follow.) Banner headlines would scream from the front pages of every newspaper and news magazine in America, "Brutal Brother-Sister Rape Shocks Community—Murder Inevitable!"

After this Absalom the son of David had a lovely sister, whose name was Tamar; and Amnon the son of David loved her. Amnon was so distressed over his sister Tamar that he became sick; for she was a virgin. And it was improper for Amnon to do anything to her. But Amnon had a friend whose name was Jonadab the son of Shimeah, David's brother. Now Jonadab was a very crafty man. And he said to him, "Why are you, the king's son, becoming thinner day after day? Will you not tell me?" Amnon said to him, "I love Tamar, my brother Absalom's sister." So Jonadab said to him, "Lie down on your

bed and pretend to be ill. And when your father comes to see you, say to him, 'Please let my sister Tamar come and give me food, and prepare the food in my sight, that I may see it and eat it from her hand'"
(2 Samuel 13:1-5 NKJV).

This was a crime of lust. Love waits, but lust can't wait! Lust says, "I have to have you now!" Love says, "I'll wait until the time is right in the sight of God."

Amnon became frustrated to the point of illness over his half-sister Tamar. Perhaps the sin in his heart would have stopped there, but then came the "friend," the demonic facilitator and cousin-in-crime that the Bible calls "a very shrewd man." Watch your friends. Do they take you higher toward Christ or pull you lower toward shame?

This friend, Jonadab, played the compassionate confidante to perfection. "Why do you, the king's son, look so haggard morning after morning? Come on, you can trust me." Then Amnon finally admitted what would be unthinkable to most normal people. "I'm in love with Tamar, my half-sister...the one who is full sister to Absalom."

In an instant, a diabolical plot hatched in Jonadab's deviant mind. "Go to bed and pretend to be sick. When your father comes to see you, tell him this...." Amnon's friend and shrewd associate, Jonadab, set up the scenario; but it was Amnon who carried it out.

BEWARE THE
JONADABS IN LIFE

Jonadab is the one who makes reservations for you at the hotel.

Jonadab is the one who "understands" that your marriage is troubled, and he reassures you that your "needs" are totally legitimate and that they "must" have an outlet, so he provides you with somebody on the side.

Jonadab *looks* as if he is converted. He *looks* like he's saved, but Jonadab is a wolf in sheep's clothing.

Jonadab is a sinner! Jonadab is a thief! Jonadab is a shrewd criminal!

Jonadab is the one who looks lightly on your fornication and adultery!

Jonadab is the one who always seems to "understand" (and condone) your mess! (Beware his motives.)

He hides you. He lowers the car seat so you can slip out of sight or conceals your honey on the side when you come around the saints.

Jonadab is the one who hides your secret.

Jonadab won't let anyone know that you are married, or that you are in adultery.

Jonadab is the one who hides your mess without regard for what God says is best.

You see numerous Jonadabs scattered throughout our churches! The problem is that a Jonadab may be *in the church* but he is not *in Christ*—his life is living proof. He may have religion, but he doesn't have a relationship with Jesus Christ. He may have a position, but he has no genuine power or anointing!

AVOID ANYONE WHO HIDES ADULTERY OR CONCEALS SIN

Beware of Jonadab! Watch those who you choose as friends. Beware of anyone who always sides with your "mess." Anyone who consents to hide adultery or conceal sin is no friend at all!

The Bible says Amnon's lust got the best of him. Stop confusing lust with love! Lust says, "I'll do whatever I need to do to get her in my bed!" Love says, "I'll wait. I will respect her and wait until the time is right!"

Then Amnon said to Tamar, "Bring the food into the bedroom, that I may eat from your hand." And Tamar took the cakes which she had made, and brought them to Amnon her brother in the bedroom. Now when she had brought them to him to eat, he took hold of her and said to her, "Come, lie with me, my sister." But she answered him, "No, my brother, do not force me, for no such thing should be done in Israel. Do not do this disgraceful thing! "And I, where could I take my shame? And as for you, you would be like one of the fools in Israel. Now therefore, please speak to the king; for he will not withhold me from you." However, he would not heed her voice; and being stronger than she, he forced her and lay with her (2 Samuel 13:10-14 NKJV).

HE HAD LUST TO SATISFY
AT ANY COST

Amnon refused to listen because he had yielded to lust. Tamar was even willing to marry him and give herself to him for the rest of her life as his wife, and it would have happened fast, in all likelihood. But Amnon refused to listen—he had lust to satisfy at any cost, and love was no issue.

As is most often the case, once Amnon had her, he hated her. After he got what he thought he wanted, the Bible says Amnon "hated her." It sounds extreme, but most sex crimes are extreme.

Then Amnon hated her exceedingly, so that the hatred with which he hated her was greater than the love with which he had loved her. And Amnon said to her, "Arise, be gone!" So she said to him, "No, indeed! This evil of sending me away is worse than the other that you did to me." But he would not listen to her. Then he called his servant who attended him, and said, "Here! Put this woman out, away from me, and bolt the door behind her." Now she had on a robe of many colors, for the king's virgin daughters wore such apparel. And his servant put her out and bolted the door behind her. Then Tamar put ashes on her head, and tore her robe of many colors that was on her, and laid her hand on her head and went away crying bitterly. And Absalom her brother said to her, "Has Amnon your brother been with you? But now hold your peace, my sister. He is your brother; do not take this thing to heart." So Tamar remained desolate in her brother Absalom's house (2 Samuel 13:15-20 NKJV).

ADDING HATEFUL INSULT TO
CRIMINAL INJURY

After raping this innocent woman, Amnon the brother, the brutal rapist, actually had the gall to order his servant to *throw out* the innocent victim and *lock her out* of his house—as if *Tamar* was the guilty one! This added hateful insult to criminal injury. It only multiplied and amplified the shame Tamar felt, leaving her with no options. Her future lost, she was at least going to sound the alarm. It didn't matter whether or not people would believe her—it was the right thing to do.

There is a blueprint called the Bible, and the Bible says, "*He who finds a wife finds a good thing*" (Prov. 18:22 NKJV). The Word of God teaches us how to live, how to operate, and how to walk. Anytime we veer from the path, we risk a fall.

Tamar walked away from that violent violation in total *shame*! She ripped her robes of royalty and threw ashes on over her head as she wept in shame.

IN THE END, SHAME CAME TO
EVERYONE INVOLVED

Amnon sowed two things that would bear especially evil seed in his life, because *consequences* always seem to follow our actions. The Law of Seedtime and Harvest never lets up; it never takes a holiday—no matter how high your position or IQ. You *will* reap what you sow!

First, Amnon sowed seeds for his own death. Tamar's older brother, Absalom, was the heir to the throne of his father, David. He loved his sister and vowed to revenge her shame, and ultimately he murdered Amnon.

David was "very angry," but did nothing. Absalom obviously counted on that, and his father's failure to act only made Absalom disdain his father as "weak," and it may have helped set the stage for full-blown rebellion and the revolt against David's kingship that Absalom later instigated. In the end, shame came to everyone involved.

Many people experience shame growing up in shameful atmospheres over which they have no control. Some grow up leading a drunken, staggering, stammering parent through the neighborhood while friends look on and laugh at the antics of "the neighborhood drunk." Others suffer shame because of the sins of a drug-addicted brother or a sibling with HIV/AIDS— which was acquired, not through blood transfusion or accidental transmission, but through a publicly flaunted, perverted lifestyle.

Some feel shame over the one relative who couldn't be trusted in the family house around Christmas or Thanksgiving! (Many families have them.) Everything of value that could be carried off had to be hidden or secured to make sure *it didn't vanish!* "Be careful because Bubba, June Bug, Slick Willy, or Shequinah is in the house and *everybody* knows you can't trust them. By the way, does that run in your family?"

Then there is a shame that haunts sons and daughters because everybody knows that their father just got out of jail. Even the janitors at the school have a betting pool to see how long he'll make it before he goes right back in.

SURVIVING THE SEARING SHAME OF
CHILD ABUSE

Millions of people experience searing shame because of the abuse they endured as a child. They have dealt with years of dodging embarrassing questions and developing inventive explanations for the deep bruises on their arms and legs. Sometimes they endure a lifetime of troubling dreams and broken relationships.

Then there is the supposedly "unmentionable" shame surrounding the "family secret"—incest. Your uncle touched you; your father touched you; your cousin and brother touched you; or even your mother touched you! Shame!

Many suffer a less intense, yet still painful shame after being forced to move away from the "right" neighborhood—the right house with the nice lawn, the nice trees, and the nice shrubs—and into the projects because Daddy or Mamma left, or because Daddy lost his job.

THE MERCY OF
GOD

Shame most often enters our lives because of sins we've committed or through unresolved issues from the past. There's a shame that we feel because of our own sin, our own mistakes, our own self-destructive behavior.

The Bible is filled with people who fell into sin or lived in shame because of the sins of others! From cover to cover, we find people who completely blew it, lost their way, gave up, lost their way back to God, and seemingly lost their way to the future. Yet somehow, by the mercy of God, they found their way back home to the Father. Through the mercy of Jesus Christ, they were restored and re-commissioned to finish what they were born to do.

If you forget everything else that I say in this chapter, then remember this: *You simply don't have time for the shame!*

YOU SIMPLY DON'T HAVE TIME
FOR THE SHAME!

What do you do with your shame? I have good news. This book was written to help you navigate your way back from the memory of the shameful and despicable things that so many still wear like a permanent garment. *There is a way back from shame.* There is a way back from disappointment. God is still at work 24 hours a day, 7 days a week, forgiving sin and having mercy *on people who need it!*

(If you don't need God's mercy, then perhaps you know someone who does. If you don't qualify on either count, then you probably don't need this book!)

The Lord is still calling in His prodigals. He is still embracing His fallen Davids and broken Peters. And He is still rebuking and driving away the religious zealots who would stone a fallen woman even before she could access the well of God's forgiveness, salvation, and restoration.

ENDNOTES

1. In Luke 9:62, Jesus warned a would-be disciple who wanted to delay his obedience to God's call, *"No man, having put his hand to the plough, and looking back, is fit for the kingdom of God."*

2. This information was derived from the work of James Strong, *Strong's Exhaustive Concordance of the Bible* (Peabody, MA: Hendrickson Publishers, n.d.). According to Dr. James Strong, there are 100 mentions of shame in the King James Version of the Bible. In addition, there are four mentions of "shamed," one mention of "shamefacedness," two mentions of "shameful," four mentions of "shamefully," one mention of "shamelessly," and two mentions of "shamer."

3. Ibid. The Hebrew terms translated as "shame" are H8103, *shimtsah*; H3637, *kalamp*; H2781, *cherpah*; H1322, *bosheth*; H3639, *kelimmah*; H954, *buwsh*; H2659, *chapher*; H7036, *qalown*; H2616, *chacad*; H6172, *ervah*; H3640, *kelimmuwth*; and H1317, *boshnah*. The Greek words translated "shame" are G152, *aischune*; G818, *atimazo*; G1788, *entrepo*; G149, *aischron*; G 819, *atimia*; G2617, *kataischuno*; G3856, *paradeigmatizo*; and G808, *aschemosune*.

4. *Merriam-Webster's Collegiate Dictionary, 10th ed.* (Springfield, MA: Merriam-Webster, Incorporated, 1994), s.v "shame."

CHAPTER NOTES

Chapter 2

ARRESTED BY SHAME

SHAME paralyzes *everyone* (including you and me). It doesn't matter whether we fall victim to shame undeserved and unasked for, or simply reap the shame we sowed through shameful deeds and wrong decisions. The effects of this paralysis by shame are usually *temporary*.

Do you remember the rush of adrenaline that exploded through your body the moment you were *caught in the act* during a childhood transgression? Your fingers tingled, your ears felt red-hot, your throat tightened, and every muscle seemed to tense up. But it all gradually drained away and a sense of "normal" ultimately returned.

Once the paralysis of exposure subsides, *many shamed sinners are tempted to return to the same sins that shamed them*. The colorful word picture of a dog "returning to his vomit" is used in both the Old and New Testaments to describe this deadly human phenomenon. (See Proverbs 26:11 and Second Peter 2:22.)

Peter, the standout apostle who personally experienced the searing shame of betrayal and cowardice, wrote to us:

For if after they have escaped the pollutions of the world through the knowledge of the Lord and Savior Jesus Christ, they are again entangled therein, and overcome, the latter end is worse with them than the beginning. For it had been better for them not to have known the way of righteousness, than, after they have known it, to turn from the holy commandment delivered unto them. But it is happened unto them according to the true proverb, the dog is turned to his own vomit again; and the sow that was washed to her wallowing in the mire (2 Peter 2:20-22).

The paralysis of shame may soon wear off, but as Christians, we should be thankful when we find ourselves *arrested* by the long arm of shame. It is the mercy and grace of God in action! It has been called "the *severe mercy* of God," and the motives of this mercy are (1) the restoration of that which has been lost, (2) the renewal of that which has worn down or lost its fire, and (3) reconciliation with those who have been separated or severed through sin.

Sin loves darkness and avoids the light at all cost. Yet, the Bible says, "*All things work together for good to them that love God, to them who are the called according to His purpose*" (Rom. 8:28).

God sees to it that *His* family members are "always caught" while others seem to get away with crime after crime. Through His severe mercy, He literally uses our wrongdoing and faults to draw us back to Him. This odd union of God's redeeming virtue and our human and satan-induced sin occurs solely through the Lord's tender mercy to us!

When you're entangled, caught-up, and exposed in the muck and mire of a secret sin, your Savior causes your shame to arrest you and presents you with a choice: repent and get better, or hide, lie, or run and get bitter.

We *all* face this choice each time we sin because none of us is perfect. I'm not sure what the public's opinion may be about the Bible, but in all of my research, I've found only *one perfect Person* connected with the Church, and it was the *religious* people of the day who *crucified Him!*

The Bible is populated with real people—imperfect people who lived in an imperfect world, and who faced many of the same pressures we face today. In page after page of Holy Scripture, we see brutally honest, full-color portraits of flawed leaders and followers who were arrested by shame in full view of God and man after their hidden sins were exposed. Their legacy in history depends upon their choice of action after their arrest. Some made good choices and became models of godly living, while many others made devastating choices and became vivid examples to later generations of the terrible wages of sin.

FEAR PRODUCES PANDERING PAWNS OF PUBLIC OPINION

Two of the greatest living examples of men arrested by shame in the Bible are permanently linked in my mind to God's purposes and biblical history: King Saul and King David. Samuel the prophet anointed Saul and named him Israel's first king. But when Saul's weakness for pleasing people led to public disobedience to the command of God, the prophet publicly confronted him with his sin.

The "fear of man" is a terrible thing. It turns brave men into cowards, and men of principle into pandering pawns of public opinion. No one should aspire to lead in the Body of Christ or in public service who is subject to the fear of man. Saul's life establishes the inescapable truth that *the fear of man* and *the fear of God* are absolutely incompatible.

The divine command given to Saul was simple and to the point—perhaps too blunt for today's politically correct church-goers: "*Now go and smite Amalek, and utterly destroy all that they have, and spare them not; but slay both man and woman, infant and suckling, ox and sheep, camel and ass*" (1 Sam. 15:3). Yet Saul disobeyed God's command.

Even before the prophet reached the scene of the crime, on the very day of Saul's sin, God described in detail how Israel's king had sinned. The portrait of compromise was so sickening to the man of God that he wept continuously until sunrise (see 1 Sam. 15:11). The following day Samuel confronted the leader he had set into office:

And Samuel came to Saul: and Saul said unto him, Blessed be thou of the Lord: I have performed the commandment of the Lord. And Samuel said, What meaneth then this bleating of the sheep in mine ears, and the lowing of the oxen which I hear? And Saul said, They have brought them from the Amalekites: for the people spared the best of the sheep and of the oxen, to sacrifice unto the Lord thy God; and the rest we have utterly destroyed (1 Samuel 15:13-15).

Did you notice King Saul's reaction to the *paralysis of shame?* If he was embarrassed at "being caught," it barely showed. He deftly shifted blame to the people while taking all of the credit for "utterly destroying" things himself.

Saul had no genuine remorse over his sin. He seemed to feel totally justified in his "modification" of God's plan. Rather than choosing honesty and the freedom produced by candid confession, Saul chose to *justify* his sin and attempted to divert blame for the sin onto the people of Israel. When Samuel questioned him, he made even more pointed statements of blame toward the people while justifying his own actions.

A genuine shepherd places himself in harm's way to protect or redeem the sheep. Saul's actions bore all the marks of a hireling, of a would-be leader who chose self-preservation over the well-being of those in his charge. In stark contrast, a true shepherd would rather place the blame for sin upon himself and spare his flock! A genuine shepherd places himself in harm's way to protect or redeem the sheep.

This is why Jesus told His disciples:

> *But he that is an hireling, and not the shepherd, whose own the sheep are not, seeth the wolf coming, and leaveth the sheep, and fleeth: and the wolf catcheth them, and scattereth the sheep. The hireling fleeth, because he is an hireling, and careth not for the sheep. I am the good shepherd, and know My sheep, and am known of Mine. As the Father knoweth Me, even so know I the Father: and I lay down My life for the sheep* (John 10:12-15).

HEART-SEARING WORDS FOR
ISRAEL'S PEOPLE-PLEASING KING

Since the temporary paralysis of shame failed to make any headway in Saul's life, God *arrested* Saul in his lie, using the iron-clad consequences of his act of disobedience and rebellion. The prophet delivered these heart-searing words of correction to Israel's people-pleasing king:

> *And Samuel said, "Hath the Lord as great delight in burnt offerings and sacrifices, as in obeying the voice of the Lord? Behold, to obey is better than sacrifice, and to hearken than the fat of rams. For rebellion is as the sin of witchcraft, and stubbornness is as iniquity and idolatry. Because thou hast rejected the word of the Lord, He hath also rejected thee from being king"* (1 Samuel 15:22-23).

Saul lived the rest of his days in pretense, falsehood, and ever-growing rebellion and hardness of heart. There were moments when Saul openly admitted his sin and confessed that David was doing the right thing. In the end, however, the seed of disobedience that Saul sowed by sparing the king of the Amalekites produced a harvest of death in his own life and family. According to the Bible, it was a young *Amalekite*, a soldier from the race Saul had been commanded to totally destroy, who actually killed Israel's king in the end (see 2 Sam. 1:1-15).

God called David *"a man after Mine own heart"* (Acts 13:22) despite the fact that he sinned against God and man a number of times. His "rap sheet" would have placed him at the top of the popular gossip columns and "tattler shows" today! David was an adulterer, a murderer in the first degree (because the murder was premeditated and carried out through accomplices), a liar, and a poor father.

DAVID DEMONSTRATED GENUINE
REMORSE AND REPENTANCE

Yet, each time David sinned against the Lord (which happened more than once), he reacted differently than Saul did. David was *arrested by shame* through the mercy of God. Confronted with the truth, David demonstrated genuine remorse and repentance, often accompanied by fasting and prayer.

As a young man, David made a mistake when he lied to the priest of Nob, concealing the fact that he was running for his life from King Saul. As a result, Saul ordered the ruthless slaughter of every priest, family member, and animal in the city of Nob. (See First Samuel 21:1-9, 22:9-23.)

After Saul's death, David presumptuously announced that he would award the leadership of his army to the boldest and the best soldier—without any regard for the person's character as a follower of God. Joab won the contest. He was the son of Zeruiah, David's half sister (see 1 Chron. 11:6). Joab's bloody ways cost David much grief during his reign as Israel's king. Later, David said this about Joab and his two brothers who also served as generals in Israel's army: "*And I am this day weak, though anointed king; and these men the sons of Zeruiah be too hard for me: the Lord shall reward the doer of evil according to his wickedness*" (2 Sam. 3:39).

But it was David's mid-life affair with Bathsheba that cost him most dearly. The unthinkable happened after David had obtained all the successes of life. The story is familiar even to people who don't consider themselves church-goers.

King David stayed home when he should have "gone to work" at the war front. The Bible says, "...*at the time when kings go forth to battle*," Israel's greatest king decided to play hooky (2 Sam. 11:1). It was almost inevitable: David found himself idle and bored.

(God did not wire men to sit around idly all day while other men work, plan, risk, and conquer obstacles and enemies. There is wisdom behind the folk saying, "Idleness is the devil's workshop"!)

In previous years, David would scan his enemy's battle lines for strengths and weaknesses. On this day, he began to scan the rooftops and windows of his city like some royal voyeur on a mission.

His wandering eyes fell on beautiful Bathsheba as she bathed on her private veranda. (They didn't have showers at that time.) By the time David discovered her identity, temptation had transformed into lust, and he took another fateful step toward tragedy. King David sent his servant with a royal summons for Bathsheba to come to the king's chambers, and Bathsheba went home pregnant.

Sin Forces You
to Live a Lie

It was bad enough that David committed adultery with Bathsheba, but then he had to cover it up as well. The problem is that once you commit a sin (and fail to confess it and repent immediately), then you have to cover it up with another sin. That leads to yet *another* sin—and another—unless you get things right with God. Sin forces you to live a lie while you make your way to the final wage of sin: death!

At first, King David tried to wait things out while setting up Bathsheba's husband to think the child was his. The problem was that Bathsheba's husband wasn't simply another stick figure among King David's hundreds of thousands of male subjects. He was Uriah the Hittite, one of the king's famous "Mighty Men" (see 2 Sam. 23:24,39). He was a man of impeccable integrity and personal discipline, a seasoned man of war who was fiercely loyal to his king, to Joab the commander (whom he served as armor-bearer), and to his fellow soldiers.

LUST AND SHAME CONSPIRED TO COMMISSION A FATAL BETRAYAL

Uriah was a trusted member of the king's elite royal bodyguard, a top leader, and a hero in the army of Israel. This man had sworn his loyalty to David in covenant; and for all of David's life until this point in time, it had been a *two-way covenant*. It seems that lust and shame conspired to rewrite the agreement and commission a fatal betrayal. The celebrated "Psalmist of Israel" was about to do something unspeakable.

What followed was so far removed from the character of the beloved Psalmist of Israel who worshiped in the sheep fields and battled Goliath in the valley of Elah (see 1 Sam. 17) that it boggles the mind. How could such a great man, an intimate friend of God, stoop so low and act so rashly with such coldhearted premeditation? James the apostle accurately describes the reason for the fall: *"But every man is tempted, when he is drawn away of his own lust, and enticed. Then when lust hath conceived, it bringeth forth sin: and sin, when it is finished, bringeth forth death"* (James 1:14-15).

In the beginning, David's deceptive scheme seemed mild, but even he didn't realize that premeditated murder lurked only a few fateful decisions away. The king disguised his first cover-up attempt as a royal inquiry into Uriah's welfare.

Immediately after Bathsheba sent word to David that she was pregnant, the king asked Joab, his general, to send home Uriah the Hittite with a report about the war. After some small talk about the soldiers and the war, David dropped a hint to Uriah:

And David said to Uriah, "Go down to thy house, and wash thy feet." And Uriah departed out of the king's house, and there followed him a mess of meat from the king. But Uriah slept at the door of the king's house with all the servants of his lord, and went not down to his house (2 Samuel 11:8-9).

Uriah was an honorable man in a very dishonorable situation. Up to this point under David's rule, no soldier of Israel had been sent to discuss the progress of a war with him *in Jerusalem*, far from the war front.

If you don't know what you're here to do, then just do some GOOD.

— Maya Angelou

Euclid Public Library

URIAH SIMPLY DID HIS DUTY...
WHILE HIS KING FORSOOK HIS

David was a warrior king, a leader who could always be found where the action was the hottest. Uriah was probably at a loss in this situation, so he simply did what he had been taught was his duty—a king *normally* would have done the same thing. Uriah didn't go home or come near Bathsheba at all, to the king's dismay.

David's plan had failed and desperation set in. He confronted Uriah in disbelief, only to receive a soldier's honorable answer:

And Uriah said unto David, "The ark, and Israel, and Judah, abide in tents; and my lord Joab, and the servants of my lord, are encamped in the open fields; shall I then go into mine house, to eat and to drink, and to lie with my wife? As thou livest, and as thy soul liveth, I will not do this thing" (2 Samuel 11:11).

The king's surrender to lust led to the commission of a sin that could not easily be covered up—especially when God Himself was determined to bring his hidden sins into the light. Yet David had one last hope: that Uriah might give in and go home before returning to the front lines, so he bought some time with a two-day delay.

THE PARALYSIS OF SHAME GAVE WAY TO
A DESPERATE SCHEME

The initial paralysis of shame was wearing off, and King David's growing fear of public exposure quickly drove the consequences of his sin into a death spiral—everything veered out of control. In short order, the paralysis of shame gave way to a desperate scheme in David's heart to conceal sin *at any cost!*

The king invited Uriah to dine with him and saw to it that his guest became drunk. Yet even in that state, Uriah refused to go home to Bathsheba. He insisted on sleeping at the palace entrance.

Sin, when it has been conceived, brings forth death! (See James 1:15.)

In desperation, David conceived of a cold-blooded scheme to cover his sin of adultery with the cloak of another sin—premeditated murder! In an act rarely matched in brutality and cruelty—even in the annals of modern Mafia or street gang warfare—the king literally asked Uriah to personally deliver a secret royal dispatch to General Joab. That dispatch called for the death of its deliverer—Uriah!

THE DEATH CONTRACT WAS EXECUTED WITH COLD-BLOODED PRECISION

Joab, the brutal soldier known for his utter ruthlessness and loyalty only to his own career, executed David's contract on Uriah's life with cold-blooded precision. He calmly ordered Uriah to lead a charge into the most dangerous place on the enemy's line, and then coolly pulled his troops back from Uriah's position.

An enemy weapon may have done the deed, but innocent Uriah's murder was traceable directly to the palace of the king.

When Bathsheba heard her husband had died, she mourned his death according to Jewish tradition. As soon as the mourning period was over, King David immediately moved her into the palace and married her. In due season, Bathsheba gave birth to a son.

Perhaps David began to breathe easier during those fleeting months leading up to his son's birth, but as Paul the apostle warned in Galatians 6:7, *"Be not deceived; God is not mocked: for whatsoever a man soweth, that shall he also reap."*

GOD MAKES AN ARREST

Since shame's warning had been ignored and set aside, God issued a divine arrest warrant for His wayward king. There would be no escape, no excuse, and no quarter. A guilty man was about to be exposed and judged by the Almighty God—and no hallowed hall of privilege or rank, or lofty title of earthly power could hinder or save the accused.

But the thing that David had done displeased the Lord. And the Lord sent Nathan unto David. And he came unto him, and said unto him, "There were two men in one city; the one rich, and the other poor. The rich man had exceeding many flocks and herds: But the poor man had nothing, save one little ewe lamb, which he had bought and nourished up: and it grew up together with him, and with his children; it did eat of his own meat, and drank of his own cup, and lay in his bosom, and was unto him as a daughter. And there came a traveller unto the rich man, and he spared to take of his own flock and of his own herd, to dress for the wayfaring man that was come unto him; but took the poor man's lamb, and dressed it for the man that was come to him." And David's anger was greatly kindled against the man; and he said to Nathan, "As the Lord liveth, the man that hath done this thing shall surely die: And he shall restore the lamb fourfold, because he did this thing, and because he had no pity" (2 Samuel 11:27b–12:1-6).

The next four words in the Word of God should send shivers down the spine of every man and woman who still possesses a conscience and any hint of understanding about right and wrong. The words Nathan the prophet uttered to David echo through the ages. They are the decree of divinity, the just prosecution of the guilty by the one Righteous Judge. There is no defense against this indictment, no belabored search for truth among mixed motives nor cross-examination to expose twisted and misleading testimony.

As the Scriptures tell us, *"Neither is there any creature that is not manifest in His sight: but all things are naked and opened unto the eyes of Him with whom we have to do"* (Heb. 4:13). The prophet of God provided a supernatural demonstration of this truth in Second Samuel 12:7a: *"And Nathan said to David, 'Thou art the man.'"*

CHAPTER NOTES

Chapter 3

DISCERNING THE DESOLATIONS OF GENERATIONS

W HEN I think of so many within the modern Church who seem to play with sin and promote immoral lifestyles while also naming the name of Jesus, I must say it as I see it:

We have played with God's love; we've played with God's grace.

We have used people for our own pleasure and then tossed them aside like a used washcloth.

We have squandered good opportunities, and we've played with our privilege.

When we finally obtained some degree of honor, dignity, and respect; when somehow we were given a good name; we have too often reverted back to our "put-one-over, hustling, manipulative, domineering ways" of selfish exploitation.

Our private sins have caused others to wonder publicly, "Can they really be trusted? Is she really real? Does he really mean it?"

ISRAEL'S BRIGHTEST LIGHT WAS NOW
A NATIONAL DISGRACE

The mighty King David—Israel's brightest light since Moses and Joshua led the children of Israel from captivity to the Promised Land—was now a national disgrace. Shacked up in the royal palace with blood on his hands, David, the royal felon, had no place to run and no excuse to offer. Arrested by shame, he could do nothing but listen in stunned shock to the just sentence and judgment of God on his deeds.

Thus saith the Lord God of Israel, "I anointed thee king over Israel, and I delivered thee out of the hand of Saul; And I gave thee thy master's house, and thy master's wives into thy bosom, and gave thee the house of Israel and of Judah; and if that had been too little, I would moreover have given unto thee such and such things. Wherefore hast thou despised the commandment of the Lord, to do evil in His sight? Thou hast killed Uriah the Hittite with the sword, and hast taken his wife to be thy wife, and hast slain him with the sword of the children of Ammon. Now therefore the sword shall never depart from thine house; because thou hast despised Me, and hast taken the wife of Uriah the Hittite to be thy wife." Thus saith the Lord, "Behold, I will raise up evil against thee out of thine own house, and I will take thy wives before thine eyes, and give them unto thy neighbour, and he shall lie with thy wives in the sight of this sun. For thou didst it secretly: but I will do this thing before all Israel, and before the sun" (2 Samuel 12:7b-12).

It is true that we live in the shadow of the cross. We are transformed and enfolded by the mercy and grace we received through the death and resurrection of Jesus Christ. Yet, I also know that God is *more* than mercy and grace, and He does not change. God Himself said, *"I am the Lord, I do not change"* (Mal. 3:6 NKJV). He is also holy and perfectly just.

SIN IS *LETHAL*,
AND IT'S HIGHLY CONTAGIOUS

Sin—our rebellion against and resistance to the righteous ways of God—is totally opposite from His nature. That means that sin is *lethal,* and it's highly contagious from generation to generation. We should flee from it at all cost. Although mercy and grace are available in abundance from God, we must do everything possible to avoid sin and the wrath of God that it produces.

Nathan's prophecy over David's house accurately describes what I believe Isaiah referred to when he talked about *"the desolations of many generations"* (Isa. 61:4). He says:

To appoint unto them that mourn in Zion, to give unto them beauty for ashes, the oil of joy for mourning, the garment of praise for the spirit of heaviness; that they might be called trees of righteousness, the planting of the Lord, that He might be glorified. And they shall build the old wastes, they shall raise up the former desolations, and they shall repair the waste cities, the desolations of many generations (Isaiah 61:3-4).

The Hebrew word translated as *desolations* means "to stun, grow numb, to devastate, stupefy, make amazed, be astonied, to be an astonishment, to make desolate, be destitute, destroy, waste, to wonder."[1] What generation comes to mind when you read these words?

THE MOMENTUM OF SIN
PRODUCES DISASTROUS CHAIN REACTIONS

No matter what we hope or wish for, the consequences of our sins simply cannot be limited to our lives alone. Like continually expanding ripples in a pool of water, the shock waves of sin's consequences affect virtually everyone who is even remotely connected to us! The momentum of sin seems to propel them from generation to generation in continuously disastrous "cause and effect" chain reactions.

The father who commits a felony and is sentenced to prison discovers that he shares his sentence with his sons and daughters—whether he likes it or not. Without a dad and provider on the scene, they will suffer the consequences of lack and feelings of abandonment and helplessness. It will happen just as surely as if they were serving time with him behind bars. The void created by his absence and the public stigma of his private sin will brand his seed with the scars of sin.

The promiscuous young woman who risks possible death or physical scarring from the rising epidemic of sexually transmitted diseases *also* risks transferring the spiritual and habitual DNA of promiscuity to her children (*if* they survive the precarious journey through a scarred and abused womb and a diseased cervix). Her liaisons outside of the marriage covenant may well doom any children she bears to life without a covenant father. Children deserve more than a childhood wasted at the mercy and whim of a male who is committed to little more than sexual pleasure and selfish satisfaction at the expense of whoever is closest at the moment. You might as well bring a sexual predator into your home and call him "Daddy."

FROM ENSLAVEMENT TO A SELF-PERPETUATING CURSE

As an African-American pastor in a major urban environment, I constantly confront the "slave mentality" in all of its modern forms. What began as the travesty of enslavement against free-born members of my ethnic group has now mutated into a lifestyle, mind-set, and devilish self-perpetuating curse. Whether you call it "entitlement thinking" or "life in the welfare dependency rut," it is a vicious cycle that is difficult to break—sometimes even for born-again Christians.

First, we must discern the *desolation* at work in our lives and families—whether we are of African-American descent or Scotch-Irish-American heritage. Second, we must harness a strong desire for change with the strongest "change agents" ever unleashed on creation: the name of Jesus, the blood of Jesus, and the Word of God.

There is eternal hope and absolute power in the truth of the cross and through the blood of Jesus. We must understand the serious consequences of sin, but not at the cost of losing our faith in the resurrection power of Jesus' sacrifice at Calvary and His victory over the grave.

I've seen countless numbers of single mothers, crack-daddies, and fatherless children rise above their circumstances and become leaders through the power of Christ and the force of their choice. Yes, sin has its consequences; but the cross *will* have the final victory in every life that is fully surrendered to Christ.

What form of desolation has come down through the generations to plague you and your children? Do you labor under the fear that you will follow the path of Aunt Tara or Uncle Willie? Do you worry that the fate of your father or your grandmother will fall upon you?

Do you fear cancer, mental illness, financial ruin, or abandonment? Does a cloud labeled "multiple sclerosis, diabetes, or Sickle Cell Anemia" overshadow every plan you try to make for the future? Do you fear your marriage will crumble in the same way that your mother's three previous marriages did?

REVERSE THE CURSE THROUGH THE POWER OF CHRIST

These are "the desolations of many generations." They are curses decreed over our lives, and often they are born out of the consequences of our own sin. The truth is that we can reverse the curse through the power of Christ and the cross. But if we don't, then the *desolations* of our sin may gain the power to stun, make numb, devastate, stupefy, make amazed, astonish and make an astonishment, make desolate and destitute, destroy and waste, and cause to wonder.

After Nathan confronted King David at God's command, we find David heartbroken over his sin and its consequences. The Psalmist was even more crushed by his broken relationship with the God of Israel.

DAVID REACHED HIS PINNACLE AT THE POINT OF ABSOLUTE FAILURE

It was there at the lowest and darkest moment of his life that David returned to his one place of hope and refuge. It might be said that David reached his pinnacle of life in God at the point of absolute failure and utter shame. As he mourned the death of his dreams and returned to God in repentance, David most epitomized "a man after God's own heart."

This isn't an encouragement to sin; it is an encouragement to *stay* in your place of hope and refuge in His presence—that way you can avoid the sorrow and consequences David had to endure.

Guilty, arrested by shame, and seemingly disqualified and moved beyond all hope for redemption, *David openly confessed his sin.* He pressed into the mercy of God in the face of the total tragedy created through his sin. The prophet had already warned him that his infant son would not live, but David did the only thing he knew to do. He laid everything before the Lord—his life, his son, his sin, his sorrow, and his longing for restoration.

And David said unto Nathan, "I have sinned against the Lord." And Nathan said unto David, "The Lord also hath put away thy sin; thou shalt not die. Howbeit, because by this deed thou hast given great occasion to the enemies of the Lord to blaspheme, the child also that is born unto thee shall surely die." And Nathan departed unto his house. And the Lord struck the child that Uriah's wife bare unto David, and it was very sick. David therefore besought God for the child; and David fasted, and went in, and lay all night upon the earth. And the elders of his house arose, and went to him, to raise him up from the earth: but he would not, neither did he eat bread with them. And it came to pass on the seventh day, that the child died (2 Samuel 12:13-18a).

Even the New Testament warns us that leaders pay a high price and are expected to follow a higher road than those who follow. Why? It is because they set the example. James the apostle said, "*My brethren* [brothers and sisters, NLT], *be not many masters* [teachers, NASB], *knowing that we shall receive the greater condemnation* [will be judged more strictly, NLT]" (James 3:1).

Nathan the prophet made it clear that God had forgiven David, but that some of the inevitable consequences would remain. The child died, and some of the other consequences affecting David's children would plague his house throughout history *until* Christ, the Great Redeemer, entered the earth through David's family line.

The good news is that no matter how terrible things may appear, there is salvation for the shamed and deliverance for the damned—if only they will *turn their heart* in repentance toward Jesus!

STUNNED BY LAWLESSNESS, STUPEFIED BY SUBSTANCE ABUSE

This is the hope we offer to our desolated generations today. We've watched entire classes and groups of people become devastated by sin, stunned by lawlessness, and stupefied by drug and substance abuse. In many cases, it seems the Church stood idly by as multitudes living around hundreds of thousands of church buildings were numbed by sorrow and destroyed and wasted by lifestyles of rebellion and blind pleasure-seeking.

Do you see evidence of desolation in your life? Has shame stolen the dream, crushed the hope, and destroyed the future of your family members and friends? Take this to heart, or tell the brokenhearted whom you love, *"You don't have to walk around in shame* because of a past sin or an indiscretion in your life! Of course it would be better if the sin had never happened, but it *did!* Repent and throw yourself on the mercy and grace of God!"

Examine the lives of the great deliverers and heroes of the Bible. With the exception of Jesus Christ, *all of them* were flawed human beings who had *sinned.* In fact, many of them appear to have been *world-class sinners* disqualified by shame! *But God...*

Noah was called a righteous man, but he got drunk on new wine after surviving the great deluge, and one of his sons boldly exposed his nakedness—which led to a curse on multiple generations of that son's descendants! (See Genesis 9:20-26.)

Abraham is honored as the father of faith, yet he also played the role of the cowardly husband when he passed off his extremely beautiful wife, Sarah, as his sister to save his own life. Abraham also grew impatient while waiting for the fulfillment of God's promise to give him a son, so he went for Sarah's "do-it-yourself Plan B." He fathered Ishmael through Hagar, and Ishmael's descendants haunt and harass the descendants of his true son, Isaac (the Jews), to this day! (See Genesis 12:11-13; Genesis 16; and Genesis 21.)

Isaac's youngest son, *Jacob,* was a con man and trickster who stole his own brother's birthright and lived life on the run. Years later, when returning home, Jacob sent his wives and children ahead to meet his angry brother who was approaching with armed men while he hid out alone and wrestled with God. (See Genesis 32:1-32.)

Moses murdered an Egyptian, was rejected by his own people, and ran for his life. He married Zipporah, a woman of color and the daughter of a priest. Moses finally returned to lead the Israelites to the Promised Land at the age of 80 after an encounter with God at the burning bush. (See Exodus 2:11–7:7.)

Samson was a tragic hero whose life reads like a comedy of errors, a flawed leader without a moral compass. At the "bottom of the barrel," blinded, ridiculed, and recognized as the laughing-stock of his race, God answered his prayer and restored him, so he could lay down his life to free his people from Philistine oppression. (See Judges 13-16.)

Gideon was another unlikely hero who stood out for his early reluctance to take risks or pay the price of leadership. It took the *patience of God* to gently coax this nay-saying, excuse-making anti-hero onto the stage of divine destiny. In the end, he led an impossibly small force against an incredibly large army, armed only with oil lamps, clay jars, and a shout to God. (See Judges 6:11–11:22.)

Peter's mistakes, gaffes, and sin of betrayal are legendary. He was impulsive, moody, presumptuous, and yet full of faith at times! (See all three Gospels plus Galatians 2:11-14.)

James and *John*, the so-called "sons of thunder," sparked controversy among the disciples through their bold covetousness for the best positions and the most honor among men. (See Mark 10:35-45.) Yet in the end, they were faithful to the Lord as apostles and witnesses to His death and resurrection.

Paul the apostle was first recognized by the infant Church as Saul the murderer and ruthless henchman of the Sanhedrin. But God managed to restore and use him mightily *anyway*. (See Acts 8:1-3; 9:1-31.)

Failure, sin, and mistakes happen in *every life* in some form or another. The best part about the lives of the biblical leaders in this list is "the rest of the story." Every one of these leaders *overcame* their obstacles. Through God's power, they repented and then *set aside their shame* over sin through their obedience. And they did it despite the desolation seeking to destroy them and the generations to follow.

We still enjoy the benefits of their breakthroughs today! Whose future will depend on *your* determination and commitment to break through the shame of your failures, falls, and sins today? You *can* find your way back from shame!

ENDNOTE

1. *Strong's*, 8074, *shamem*, shaw-mame'; a prim. root; to stun (or intrans. grow numb), i.e. devastate or (fig.) stupefy (both usually in a passive sense):—make amazed, be astonied, (be an) astonish (-ment), (be, bring into, unto, lay, lie, make) desolate (-ion, places), be destitute, destroy (self), (lay, lie, make) waste, wonder.

CHAPTER NOTES

Chapter 4

You Can Find Your Way Back From Shame!

*T*WO *men* betrayed Jesus on the same fateful day. One man betrayed Him with a kiss, the other with a curse. Both men were paralyzed and arrested by shame. One of them took his own life in surrender to unbearable shame, but the other took on a new life in surrender to God's unmatched and unconditional love.

These men walked together, talked together, ate together, prayed for the sick, and cast out demons together. They heard the same sermons and teachings, witnessed the same miracles, and looked into the eyes of the same Savior. These men shared a communal life with Jesus for approximately 42 months, experiencing the most supernatural intervention in the affairs of men the earth had ever known. Then *what they both viewed as a crisis* abruptly ended their relationship and miraculously altered the world.

Judas Iscariot was the smart one. We assume he was the educated one, too. After all, the Bible tells us he was the disciple
entrusted to handle the money for the traveling ministry team. It
seems that Judas looked after the "practical" things. His problems
began with a faulty moral foundation, but they came to a head
the day he concluded that Jesus' mission and message just weren't
practical, and somebody had to "do something."

Peter the fisherman was the impulsive one. He was the water-
walker, the loud-talker, the front-runner, and the sword-swinger.
From the beginning, it seemed Peter had become the apparent
leader among the twelve disciples through force of personality
and passion.

THREE POINTS OF HOPE IN
A NIGHT OF FAILURE

Three things stand out about Peter's failure before Christ's
crucifixion and his process of restoration. They offer unshakable
hope to anyone who has failed in life.

*And the Lord said, "Simon, Simon, behold, Satan hath desired to
have you, that he may sift you as wheat: But I have prayed for thee,
that thy faith fail not: and when thou art converted, strengthen thy
brethren." And he said unto Him, "Lord, I am ready to go with Thee,
both into prison, and to death." And He said, "I tell thee, Peter, the
cock shall not crow this day, before that thou shalt thrice deny that
thou knowest Me"* (Luke 22:31-34).

1. Jesus *knew*.

The Lord knew Peter would fall. He publicly warned Peter about his fiery trial before it ever happened, and the disciple *understood enough to deny that it would ever happen.* (Yet, *all four Gospels* tell us it *did* happen).

> *Peter answered and said unto Him, "Though all men shall be offended because of Thee, yet will I never be offended." Jesus said unto him, "Verily I say unto thee, That this night, before the cock crow, thou shalt deny Me thrice." Peter said unto Him, "Though I should die with Thee, yet will I not deny Thee." Likewise also said all the disciples* (Matthew 26:33-35).

When Peter boldly claimed he would never deny Jesus, the other disciples chimed in to claim the same thing. (See also Mark 14:30, Luke 22:34, and John 13:38.) Jesus knew Peter's words outstripped his ability to fulfill them. Jesus knew Peter would fail. In fact, He knew *where* it would take place, *when* it would happen, and *how many times* it would occur.

The Lord wasn't caught off guard by Peter's failure, and He isn't surprised or put off by *our* failures either! He already knows where, when, and how many times you will fail too, so don't be ashamed to go to Him in honest confession and absolute trust. He loved you long before you ever knew Him or received Him as Lord.

2. Jesus *prayed*.

After Jesus gave Peter a solemn warning, He also armed him with a personal promise just before he entered the greatest struggle of his life: "*But I have prayed for thee, that thy faith fail not*" (Luke 22:32a). What an incredible promise!

How would you feel if you knew Jesus was personally praying for you? Would your attitudes change if you felt assured that your faith would never fail? Would any task seem too hard or too difficult to tackle?

Peter, himself, has something to say to you: "*Then Peter opened his mouth, and said, "Of a truth I perceive that God is no respecter of persons*" (Acts 10:34). In other words, what Jesus did for Peter *He will also do for you*!

If you still have trouble believing it, then consider this declaration about Jesus and His moment-by-moment ministry in your life: "*Wherefore He is able also to save them to the uttermost that come unto God by Him, seeing He ever liveth to make intercession for them*" (Heb. 7:25). If you came to God through Jesus, then He is interceding for you *right now*!

3. Peter *wept*.

The first two points of hope focus solely on the power and work of Jesus Christ that still go on this very moment. The third *depends totally upon you*.

Take time to carefully review the events on the night of Peter's greatest failure according to Luke's account:

Then took they Him, and led Him, and brought Him into the high priest's house. And Peter followed afar off. And when they had kindled a fire in the midst of the hall, and were set down together, Peter sat down among them. But a certain maid beheld him as he sat by the fire, and earnestly looked upon him, and said, "This man was also with Him." And he denied Him, saying, "Woman, I know Him not." And after a little while another saw him, and said, "Thou art also of them." And Peter said, "Man, I am not." And about the space of one hour after another confidently affirmed, saying, "Of a truth this fellow also was with Him: for he is a Galilaean." And Peter said, "Man, I know not what thou sayest." And immediately, while he yet spake, the cock crew. And the Lord turned, and looked upon Peter. And Peter remembered the word of the Lord, how He had said unto him, "Before the cock crow, thou shalt deny Me thrice." And Peter went out, and wept bitterly (Luke 22:54-62).

Why is it so important for Peter to weep? "*Peter, please weep* because what you've done was grievous. Your mouth was too big." (I *know* this never happens in your life, but it *certainly* happens in nearly everyone else's life). "It seems, Peter, that you were not necessarily 'God-assured,' but it is *obvious* you were too *self*-assured."

"*Peter, please weep* because you thought more highly of yourself than you ought to. You were arrogant when you should have been humble." The Bible says, "*Wherefore let him that thinketh he standeth take heed lest he fall*" (1 Cor. 10:12).

Sometimes I fear we put too much stock in our giftedness, in our anointing, and especially in our splendid spiritual pedigrees based on the way we were raised. It comes out in our mouths and shows up in our testimonies. (If you remember, Jesus warned,

"Out of the abundance of the heart the mouth speaketh" in Matthew 12:34; see also Luke 6:45.)

SPIRITUAL PEDIGREES CAN BECOME
ARROGANT DISPLAYS

"Well, don't you know we came from the 'sanctified' church? I've been sanctified since I was 15 and preaching since I was 18! I've been ordained since I was 21, and I've been a pastor for 20 years."

If you are not careful, your splendid spiritual pedigree can become an arrogant display of hypocrisy! Your proud words of arrogant religiosity can make other people feel that you believe you are beyond sin.

If you ask me, one of the most frightening warnings in the Bible appears in Proverbs 16:18: *"Pride goeth before destruction, and an haughty spirit before a fall."*

Peter was what we would call "a man's man." He was a fisherman, a blue-collar worker with rough, work-hardened hands and sun-ravaged skin. He was rough and rugged around the edges, and he was edgy and ready for a fight most of the time. He even drew a sword and sliced off a man's ear in the Garden of Gethsemane (see John 18:10). But all of these "manhood credentials" didn't do him much good in the heat of the *real* battle. According to the Gospels, Peter denied the Lord at the time when Jesus needed him most.

For years, I preached from the text in Luke 22, beginning with verse 54, and *ending with verse 61.* At the end of this message on Peter's failure, I often stalked through the congregation looking for "Peter." Under the title, "Heated by the Wrong Fire," I usually ended the service saying something like: "Peter, Jesus is looking for you! Talented Peter, I'm talking to you, the one with ability. Anointed Peter, I'm calling for you. Are you Backsliding Peter? Now come on to the altar."

One Sunday in particular I even ventured up into the balcony pulling every "Peter" I could find out of the pew—particularly the singing Peter, the preaching Peter, and the ministering Peter—who was arrogant.

When you are arrogant, you feel that you don't need correction. When you are corrected, then you feel that you were erroneously corrected. "After all, I've been with the Lord a long time." So what? Peter had followed the Lord for a long time too. Yet, when the Lord needed him the most, he decided to follow the Lord "afar off." *If the enemy can just get you to follow God at a distance, then it won't be long before you deny Him.*

But this time in Luke 22, the Holy Spirit has urged me to emphasize verse 62: *"Peter went out and wept bitterly"* (NKJV). Peter committed the same crime as Judas, but he reacted to the shame differently.

Judas sold out Jesus for 30 pieces of silver, an action that openly denied the Lord's identity and divine mission as the only begotten Son of God. Once Judas had convinced himself that Jesus had "gone over the top" with His claim to divinity and His determination to lay down His life for the lost, then he put action to his betrayal. Judas sold Jesus into the hands of His accusers, beginning the brutal downward spiral to our Lord's suffering and crucifixion.

Like Peter, Judas sold Jesus down the river. But unlike Peter, Judas could not find consolation in repentance. He yielded to despair and went out and hung himself.

We all deny the Christ. It happens each time we fail, sin, or disobey His commands. If you don't go out and weep bitterly, then your conscience with its guilt and despair may lead you to destruction (spiritually if not physically).

Judas died by his own hand because when he sinned against Christ, he failed to weep bitterly with *"fruits meet for repentance"* (Matt. 3:8; see also Acts 26:20). Once he realized what he had done, he *did* feel remorse. He even tried to give back the 30 pieces of silver he'd received for the betrayal, but when his offer was rejected, his repentance ended there. It seems that Judas' repentance majored on the practical, the social, and the human realm. He went to the people involved, and once he was rejected, perhaps he felt his options had been exhausted.

Peter denied Christ too—three times! Peter failed just as miserably as Judas, but Peter wept. His heartfelt sorrow and prayer of repentance released the forgiveness of God in his life.

Have you ever denied Him? Did you go where He told you not to go? Have you ever done something He told you not to do in His Word? Have you said things He told you not to say? Are you running with people He told you to stay away from? That means you have denied Him. If you're not careful, your guilt will lead you where you don't want to go!

Are you honest enough to admit that you've been guilty of these things? You know all of the stories and claims you've made about your sanctified self, so that also means that you know how difficult it is to repent and tell the truth after you've already put on a show while dressed up in all of your Sunday finery!

(It can really be embarrassing when you are guilty and everybody who knows you—especially your family members and close friends—already *knows* you are guilty.)

One of the greatest services we can do for our children is to teach them how to live honestly without cover-ups and hypocrisy. The first step in that process is to stop teaching our children shortcuts and excuse-making skills. Just tell it straight with a strong dose of love.

"You're guilty. You didn't do your homework—so you're wrong. No, I'm not going to get you out of this. No, I won't call your teacher and say you're sick. You have to learn how to make amends for yourself."

Stop making excuses for your sins and the sins of your family members. Take personal responsibility for any foolishness in your life, and help others in your life do the same. If we don't, we doom ourselves to life as professional "victims."

"It wasn't me, it was *you!*"

"I really didn't mean to fornicate. It wasn't really my fault; I mean, she started undressing. What's a guy supposed to do when a woman does that? It was not my fault."

"He was the one who rolled the joint. Everyone was watching, so I *had* to smoke with them."

"Those guys put the money on the counter right in front of me. They should have known I had a problem with money. I know I shouldn't have stolen it, but it wasn't my fault. If you are stupid enough to put money in front of me, then you deserve to lose it. I admit I have a problem, but it was *their* fault that I took the money."

The Bible says that Jesus looked over at Peter right after he had repeatedly denied Him. I can almost imagine how Peter felt when he saw "the look." Have you ever wronged people only to have them look at you in gracious forgiveness in the midst of their pain? You know you've wronged them; you've talked about them like they were trash. Yet, they still come up to you and say sincerely, "The peace of the Lord be with you."

Jesus looked at Peter, and Peter looked at Jesus. The boldest disciple was ashamed. Shame can be a good thing; holy guilt is good because it prompts us to repentance.

Peter's shame forced the issue of repentance in his life. Shame made Peter go out and weep and say, "I am sorry. I was a disciple. I was one of the three chosen, and I know that to whom much is given, much is to be required" (see Luke 12:48).

I'm sure that Andrew, Thomas, and Matthew wanted to be close to Jesus in the same way as Peter, James, and John. Yet, for whatever reason, Jesus selected Peter, James, and John for His inner circle.

Everyone wants to be a part of the inner circle of church leadership, of the corporate board of directors, or of the state government. But very few realize that life in an inner circle also has the most "hell"—high-level stress and responsibility—thrown in with the "heaven" of high-level belonging and privileged knowledge.

Remember that those who are closest to the leader have the most responsibility, endure the most jealousy, and face the most adversity. Members of the inner circle see the rough, the rugged, and the raw.

The three disciples, Peter, James, and John, saw the Savior in all of His humanity. (They didn't see *any* sin, but they *did* see unbelievable pain, sorrow, agony, and suffering.) Perhaps Andrew, Thomas, and Matthew wanted to be where Peter, James, and John were, but that was not God's design for them. Each of the Twelve was destined to follow his own God-ordained path, strewn with divine blessings, demonic opposition, earthly struggles, and heavenly rewards.

Learn to bloom and prosper where God puts you, because where God puts you is where God wants you.

Peter, James, and John all had anointing, and they genuinely loved Jesus. Peter was a talented and bold leader in his own right, yet with all of that talent, energy, and boldness, Peter denied Jesus—even though he was the first to publicly boast, "I never would deny You."

This is the point: If Peter could, then you can. If Peter could recover from sharing the spotlight with Judas for being one of the two worst betrayers ever recorded in human history, then you, too, can *find your way back from shame!*

Of course, this view doesn't fit well with the form of Christianity actually practiced in many of the hallowed halls of our churches today, but the *fact* of the matter is that God still majors on restoring people from shame, and on restoring lost prodigals to the Great Shepherd's fold!

ENDNOTES

1. *Strong's Exhaustive Concordance of the Bible,* 8074, shamem, shaw-mame'; a prim. root; to stun (or intrans. grow numb), i.e. devastate or (fig.) stupefy (both usually in a passive sense):—make amazed, be astonied, (be an) astonish (-ment), (be, bring into, unto, lay, lie, make) desolate (-ion, places), be destitute, destroy (self), (lay, lie, make) waste, wonder.

CHAPTER NOTES

Chapter 5

REMOVE THE
STUMBLING BLOCK

AN old vaudeville routine that has been reinvented thousands of times goes something like this:

"Doctor, Doctor, I'm desperate. I need your help!"

"What's wrong? Maybe I can help you."

"Well, I don't know what the problem is, but every time I move my arm like this, I get a stabbing pain right here!"

"I think I have the answer."

"I knew a great doctor like you could find the cure. Okay, tell me what to do."

"Now, you told me that every time you move your arm in that certain way, then you get a stabbing pain. Is that correct?"

"Wow! I think you've got it. So what do I do? Do you have a prescription? A procedure? A scientific discovery?"

"Yes. Don't move your arm like that."

So what does this have to do with shame? The short answer is: *Stop doing the things you were doing to produce that shame.*

Paul the apostle invested years of teaching, training, prayer, and fasting in the church at Corinth. This church was composed of mostly non-Jewish converts to Christ. They "came out of" what amounts to an incredibly accurate checklist of sins that plague millions of Christians around the world *today*.

RICH IN GIFTS,
WEIGHED DOWN IN SIN

The Corinthian church experienced fantastic growth and flowed in a rich abundance of spiritual gifts. It also wrestled with all of the baggage of sinful lifestyles, low moral standards, and the abuse of godly gifts for personal prestige or political advantage.

In his first apostolic letter to the Corinthians, Paul laid out the truth about things that produce shame and how to deal with them:

Know ye not that the unrighteous shall not inherit the kingdom of God? Be not deceived: neither fornicators, nor idolaters, nor adulterers, nor effeminate, nor abusers of themselves with mankind, Nor thieves, nor covetous, nor drunkards, nor revilers, nor extortioners, shall inherit the kingdom of God. And such were some of you: but ye are washed, but ye are sanctified, but ye are justified in the name of the Lord Jesus, and by the Spirit of our God. All things are lawful unto me, but all things are not expedient: all things are lawful for me, but I will not be brought under the power of any (1 Corinthians 6:9-12).

The New Living Translation phrases that first line this way: *"Don't you realize that those who do wrong will not inherit the Kingdom of God? Don't fool yourselves"* (1 Cor. 6:9a NLT).

PAUL LISTED THE FAMILIAR STUMBLING BLOCKS

Paul confronted the mostly Gentile church in Galatia with a similar list of familiar stumbling blocks that included: *"adultery, fornication, uncleanness, lasciviousness, idolatry, witchcraft, hatred, variance, emulations, wrath, strife, seditions, heresies, envyings, murders, drunkenness,* [and] *revellings"* (Gal. 5:19-21a). The cultures and eras may change, but sin does not—neither does its cure.

The apostle ended with a warning: *"Let me tell you again, as I have before, that anyone living that sort of life will not inherit the Kingdom of God"* (Gal. 5:21b NLT). It doesn't get any more blunt than this.

CULTURES AND ERAS MAY CHANGE, BUT SIN DOES NOT—NEITHER DOES ITS CURE.

How many people who publicly call themselves Christians, and who dress up and go to church each Sunday, match this description of the adulterous woman of Proverbs: "*Such is the way of an adulterous woman; she eateth, and wipeth her mouth, and saith, I have done no wickedness*" (Prov. 30:20).

I'm convinced that most Bible-preaching pastors in this modern era will, at some point, have to deal with church-going, Bible-quoting folks who live together out of wedlock and think they are eligible for God's blessings. They usually claim with surprise, when confronted, "Yes, we're living together, but we aren't doing anything wrong. We *love* each other. We'll get married...*some* day."

Our churches are filled with choir members, deacons, and charter members who regularly cheat on their taxes, falsify official documents, lie on job applications or medical forms, and cheat on their spouses. And all too often, the shame trail leads directly to hidden sins in the pastor's office or church headquarters. Men and women may be fooled, but the last time I checked my Bible, it is still written in Galatians 6:7: "*Be not deceived; God is not mocked: for whatsoever a man soweth, that shall he also reap.*" God cannot—and will not—be mocked. We should pray that in His mercy, shame will drive us to repentance and restoration!

What is the remedy for our shame? How do we get right with God and put away shame once and for all? What is the most direct path to freedom?

The good news is that there is a way back from shame! There is a way to walk in the newness of life once again after you have repented of your sin, after you have shown yourself genuinely remorseful before God.

FIRST, REMOVE
THE STUMBLING BLOCK!

Paul asked the same people who received his stern warning at Galatia, "*Ye did run well; who did hinder you that ye should not obey the truth?*" (Gal. 5:7). So let me ask you something that we all need to think about from time to time: *What happened to you? What is your stumbling block?*

What repetitive sin or temptation just keeps rising to the surface to infect your daily life?

Do you get angry over the smallest of things—on a daily basis?

Are you drawn to pornography, alcohol, or drugs, with very little ability to resist them?

Do you feel "bitter" most of the time, feeling you are an undeserving victim surrounded by equally undeserving "blessed people"?

Paul said, "*Stand fast therefore in the liberty wherewith Christ hath made us free, and be not entangled again with the yoke of bondage*" (Gal. 5:1). Don't get trapped again in that vicious cycle that always locks you up and forces you to live as a slave!

Drawing upon the original Greek words used in the phrase, Paul was saying in essence, "*Don't get trapped again in that vicious cycle that always locks you up and forces you to live as a slave!*"[1]

Whatever the stumbling block may be in your life; you must remove it. This new heavenly environment of freedom was so important to Jesus that He painted us a word picture that leaves no room for argument, sidestepping, or justification. Listen to His commands about how we should deal with the stumbling blocks in our lives:

And whosoever shall offend one of these little ones that believe in Me, it is better for him that a millstone were hanged about his neck, and he were cast into the sea. And if thy hand offend thee, cut it off: it is better for thee to enter into life maimed, than having two hands to go into hell, into the fire that never shall be quenched: Where their worm dieth not, and the fire is not quenched. And if thy foot offend thee, cut it off: it is better for thee to enter halt into life, than having two feet to be cast into hell, into the fire that never shall be quenched: Where their worm dieth not, and the fire is not quenched. And if thine eye offend thee, pluck it out: it is better for thee to enter into the kingdom of God with one eye, than having two eyes to be cast into hell fire: Where their worm dieth not, and the fire is not quenched (Mark 9:42-48; see also Matthew 5:29-30).

Don't be fooled by the word "offend." You may be saying to yourself, "Well, my problem doesn't *offend* me. The problem is that I *like* it too much!" The Greek word translated as *offend* is the root for our English word, "scandalize." It really means "to entrap, trip up, stumble, or entice to sin, apostasy or displeasure, to make offensive."[2]

What is making you *offensive* to God and *to others*? In other words, Jesus is asking us, "What is tripping you up and scandalizing you? What is making you *offensive to God* and *to others*?"

Many Christians ignore God's warning and become "unequally yoked" emotionally and even physically with people in total opposition to the Kingdom of God. *Are you running with someone* who is headed toward hell at breakneck speed? Then you *must* make a choice. Remove the stumbling block or be prepared to spend eternity in hell with that unequally yoked friend!

There is one very important exception. If you are married to an unbeliever, then you must make it your aim to win them to the Lord through your godly life—but *not* through compromise.

But to the rest speak I, not the Lord: If any brother hath a wife that believeth not, and she be pleased to dwell with him, let him not put her away. And the woman which hath an husband that believeth not, and if he be pleased to dwell with her, let her not leave him. For the unbelieving husband is sanctified by the wife, and the unbelieving wife is sanctified by the husband: else were your children unclean; but now are they holy. But if the unbelieving depart, let him depart. A brother or a sister is not under bondage in such cases: but God hath called us to peace. For what knowest thou, O wife, whether thou shalt save thy husband? or how knowest thou, O man, whether thou shalt save thy wife? (1 Corinthians 7:12-16).*

Other than this, if something in your life or body is trying to kill you, if you feel bound up and can't seem to break free, then ask God to *kill it* before it kills you! I'm not telling you to issue an "angelic hit contract" on somebody—again, our warfare is not against flesh and blood but against "*principalities, against powers, against the rulers of the darkness of this world, against spiritual wickedness in high places*" according to the apostle Paul in Ephesians 6:12.

If something in your life or body is trying to kill you, if you feel bound up and can't seem to break free, then ask God to *kill it* before it kills you! When you know your life and destiny are at stake, I urge you to ask God to kill the relationship, the addiction, the unhealthy habit, or the cancer that attacks your body and soul.

As we noted earlier, Jesus told Peter the disciple, *"Simon, Simon, behold, Satan hath desired to have you, that he may sift you as wheat: But I have prayed for thee, that thy faith fail not: and when thou art converted, strengthen thy brethren"* (Luke 22:31-32).

Jesus Christ is praying for you and me this very moment, asking the Father to keep our faith alive and at work in our lives. He is praying for you, that you will remove the stumbling blocks from your life and turn around completely! He is praying that when you successfully pass through the valleys of your life, then you will strengthen others around you.

There is a way back from shame, and one of the most important actions in God's remedy for removing shame is for you to *remove the stumbling block!*

ENDNOTES

1. This expanded and rephrased passage from Galatians 5:1 was composed from elements of the following *Strong's* Greek word definitions: "1758, enecho, en-ekh'-o; from G1722 and G2192; to hold in or upon, i.e. ensnare; by impl. to keep a grudge:—entangle with, have a quarrel against, urge. 3825, palin, pal'-in; prob. from the same as G3823 (through the idea of oscillatory repetition); (adv.) anew, i.e. (of place) back, (of time) once more, or (conj.) furthermore or on the other hand:—again. 2218, zugos, dzoo-gos'; from the root of zeugnumi (to join espec. by a "yoke"); a coupling, i.e. (fig.) servitude a law or obligation); also (lit.) the beam of the balance (as connecting the scales):—pair of balances, yoke. 1397, douleia, doo-li'-ah; from G1398; slavery (cer. or fig.):—bondage. 1398, douleuo, dool-yoo'-o; from G1401; to be a slave to (lit. or fig., invol. or vol.):—be in bondage, (do) serve (-ice)."

2. Adapted from *Strong's*, Greek #4624, *skandalizo*, skan-dal-id'-zo ("scandalize"); from G4625; to entrap, i.e. trip up (fig. stumble [trans.] or entice to sin, apostasy or displeasure):—(make to) offend.

CHAPTER NOTES

Chapter 6

Renounce Everything That Is Not Like God

A married man was caught carrying on an affair with another woman, but he begged his wife not to divorce him. He reassured her that he still wanted to be married to her, and agreed to go with her to their pastor for counseling.

When confronted with the situation, the man freely admitted his sin, said he wanted to preserve his marriage and family, and then asked his wife to forgive him.

Just before the couple left the office, the pastor made a very simple and important point:

"Now you know, of course, that this means you have to give up your relationship with the other woman, don't you?"

"What? You never said anything about that! I *love* her. I'm not going to give her up too. I've already admitted that I knew it was wrong; isn't that enough?"

This sounds ridiculous, doesn't it? Something is missing from this man's thinking. You should be shocked to know that this kind of thing happens all the time among Christians as well as non-believers, but you probably aren't (because you already know it does).

Human societies habitually loosen and set aside spiritual and behavioral guidelines from generation to generation in the name of personal freedom or "deeper enlightenment." They also turn aside time-proven concepts of right and wrong when faced with strong personalities or forceful organizations pressing for particular ideas.

"WINKED AT" OR "LEGALIZED"—
WRONG IS STILL WRONG

Public drunkenness (and its modern stepchild, substance abuse), prostitution, sexual predation on women and children, and violent religious persecution have all been endorsed and publicly winked at or "legalized" in major nations and cultures—*but they are still wrong.*

Adolf Hitler declared open season on Jews, homosexuals, and the mentally challenged early in the 20th century; and many of the organized churches of Germany looked the other way or even assisted the effort to exterminate these people. It was *still wrong.* (A minority of Germany's Protestant church leaders and believers openly opposed the Nazi injustice. Some of these leaders, such as Martin Niemoeller and Karl Barth, were persecuted, exiled, or imprisoned. Pastor Dietrich Bonhoeffer was martyred for putting action to his Bible-based beliefs.[1])

The apartheid policies of South Africa officially sanctioned the mistreatment and political enslavement of people of color, and used misapplied and incorrectly interpreted Scriptures in an attempt to justify the government's pro-discrimination, racial laws. The world community, and ultimately, the government of South Africa, finally acknowledged that apartheid was wrong, but only after much bloodshed and sorrow had swept through that country.[2]

Saddam Hussein launched the "Anfal" or "Spoils" displacement campaign against the minority Kurdish people of Iraq in 1988. His cousin, General Ali Hassan al-Majid (or "Chemical Ali") used chemical weapons and other means of mass destruction to murder as many as 182,000 people according to documents, remains, and eye witnesses produced by international human rights groups.[3]

Regardless of the many varying opinions held toward the current armed conflict in Iraq, virtually everyone seems to agree that the Iraqi holocaust was *wrong*. Hussein first appeared before an Iraqi court in July of 2004 to face criminal charges for his acts of "ethnic cleansing" against Kurdish men, women, and children, and was later sentenced to death for his crimes.[4]

Unlike the continually wavering and shifting sand of human opinion, the wisdom of God has *never* been affected or influenced by the stupidity or immoral whims of humanity. If God says a thing is sin, then it is sin no matter how many names we give it. It is wrong regardless of how many volumes we write to condone it. It is unrighteous and condemned no matter how many people gather together in a vain attempt to vote it out of the sin column and into the "socially in" column.

SO SIN IS SIN—
WHAT DO YOU DO ABOUT IT?

Once you face the fact that sin is sin, and that we all have sinned (even after you accepted Jesus Christ), then what do you do about it? John the apostle was one of the most practical people in the Bible. Under the direct inspiration of God, John answered this question about real-life sin in the lives of born-again Christians when he wrote: "*My little children, these things write I unto you, that ye sin not. And if any man sin, we have an advocate with the Father, Jesus Christ the righteous*" (1 John 2:1).

The New Living Translation puts it this way: "*But if anyone does sin, we have an advocate who pleads our case before the Father*" (1 John 2:1b NLT). The problem is that we can't expect Jesus to plead our case if we are so double-minded about our sin that we will probably go out and commit the same sin again the first chance we get!

Jesus said in Matthew 3:8 that we must show "*fruits meet for repentance.*" The New Living Translation says it this way: "*Prove by the way you live that you have repented of your sins and turned to God*" (Matthew 3:8 NLT).

Since you and I are human, we must do what it takes to follow through on our decisions. The second step that should follow our honest acknowledgment of a sin is that we should openly *renounce everything that is not like God!*

You don't have to believe me just because I say so. Consult God's Word on the matter for yourself. Listen to the apostle Paul's prescription for leaders who want to please God and leave behind human weaknesses:

Therefore, since through God's mercy we have this ministry, we do not lose heart. Rather, we have renounced secret and shameful ways; we do not use deception, nor do we distort the word of God. On the contrary, by setting forth the truth plainly we commend ourselves to every man's conscience in the sight of God (2 Corinthians 4:1-2 NIV).

What does Paul mean when he uses the word, "renounce"? The original Greek word translated as *renounce* means literally "to tell from."[5] It refers to the act of openly disowning shameful things, or to forbid them. One authority says "the meaning to renounce may therefore carry with it the thought of *forbidding the approach* of the things disowned."[6]

I Don't Want That Thing Near Me!

So it seems that when we *renounce* a thing, it isn't enough for us to merely say, "This is a bad thing—I'm sorry I did it." We are actually saying, "Never again! I don't want that thing near me. Don't even think of coming close to me—you are a disgusting and revolting thing. I'll have nothing to do with you—in fact, I don't even want you to come near me! I want something better; I love Another, the One who gave all for me!"

It is time for the people of God, the Body of Christ in the earth, to rise up and loudly declare:

We renounce secret and shameful ways!

We renounce everything unclean!

We renounce generational curses!

We renounce the spirit of lust!

We renounce the spirit of poverty!

We renounce the spirit of shame!

We renounce the hidden things!

We renounce everything that is not like God!

Put everything under the blood of the Lamb! Call it by name, and *renounce* it! This is the way to break the power of bondages, addictions, and satanic entrances to your life and soul.

Freedom comes when you put bondage and sin under the blood of the Lamb and refuse to handle the Word of God in a deceptive way! Do you realize that if you are not careful and if you don't understand the Word of God by the Spirit of God, then you can be deceived and attempt to make wrong *right*!

How do you make wrong right? You say and believe that God would send a man *who is still married* to someone else. You distort God's Word when you believe that God would overlook your indiscretions while condemning the sins of others. You justify your decision to deal drugs or provide misleading numbers for your taxes by saying, "I need the money!" That is distorting the Word of God!

DECEIVING AND BEING DECEIVED: THEY GO HAND IN HAND

The Scriptures warn us about people who "go about deceiving and being deceived." It's true: These twin sisters go hand in hand.

The Scriptures also say much more about the solution to the problem:

> *Yea, and all that will live godly in Christ Jesus shall suffer persecution. But evil men and seducers shall wax worse and worse, deceiving, and being deceived. But continue thou in the things which thou hast learned and hast been assured of, knowing of whom thou hast learned them; And that from a child thou hast known the holy scriptures, which are able to make thee wise unto salvation through faith which is in Christ Jesus. All scripture is given by inspiration of God, and is profitable for doctrine, for reproof, for correction, for instruction in righteousness: That the man of God may be perfect, thoroughly furnished unto all good works* (2 Timothy 3:12-17).

Have you been deceived by a spirit that makes you feel it is all right to handle dope or lie to the IRS? Listen, even if you don't sell drugs in the street, you've become a drug king-pin in high places! Satan's imps know you by your deeds. Even if the IRS doesn't catch you, and even if the size of the lie seems small and insignificant to you, it looms large in God's eyes because it is *sin*, and it *separates* you from Him.

SIN
SEPARATES

I'm not spouting my educated ideas about what God might think. Read it for yourself directly from His Word! "*Behold, the Lord's hand is not shortened, that it cannot save; neither His ear heavy, that it cannot hear:*

But your iniquities have separated between you and your God, and your sins have hid His face from you, that He will not hear" (Isaiah 59:1-2).

If you feel compelled to twist Scripture to justify your choices or actions, then your mind has not been transformed by "the washing of the water of the Word" through the Spirit of God.[7] If you try to make wrong right and willingly warp your presentation and interpretation of the Scriptures to justify your actions, then unfortunately you have learned what it means "to handle the Word of God deceitfully"!

You know there are problems if you feel compelled to "explain" your choices or lifestyle so people will "understand" you.

"Well, it's really my culture."

"You and I both know things are not the same as they used to be."

The last time you checked, was adultery in the 21st century still the same thing as adultery in the first century? Is theft still a bad thing—do people in our "culture" still apprehend and prosecute people caught in the act of stealing? Is a lie still a lie? No, wait a minute. Could any thinking person actually *believe* the Lord of the universe will buy our modern argument that "a lie is a lie only when you can't come up with a good alibi"?

The Bible is still right! Sin is still wrong, and *God still keeps an account* of every idle word! "*But I say unto you, That every idle word that men shall speak, they shall give account thereof in the day of judgment. For by thy words thou shalt be justified, and by thy words thou shalt be condemned*" (Matthew 12:36-37).

Everyone must give an account.

But why dost thou judge thy brother? or why dost thou set at nought thy brother? for we shall all stand before the judgment seat of Christ. For it is written, As I live, saith the Lord, every knee shall bow to Me, and every tongue shall confess to God. So then every one of us shall give account of himself to God (Romans 14:10-12).

He will judge both the dead and the living.

Wherein they think it strange that ye run not with them to the same excess of riot, speaking evil of you: Who shall give account to Him that is ready to judge the quick and the dead. For for this cause was the gospel preached also to them that are dead, that they might be judged according to men in the flesh, but live according to God in the spirit. But the end of all things is at hand: be ye therefore sober, and watch unto prayer. And above all things have fervent charity among yourselves: for charity shall cover the multitude of sins (1 Peter 4:4-8).

We will *all* stand before the Judge: "*For we must all appear before the judgment seat of Christ; that every one may receive the things done in his body, according to that he hath done, whether it be good or bad*" (2 Corinthians 5:10).

Communication technology has advanced in about 150 years from "rapid" mail delivery by Pony Express to Instant Messaging and iPods; in addition, transportation exploded from the horse and buggy to public sales of tickets to outer space. Yet despite our scientific advances, the human race continues its relentless slide into moral and spiritual decline. Such is "modern" life apart from God's presence and perfect plan.

"Yes, I repented of sin, but it just seems to keep popping up in my life and in my family."

You must *renounce* and forbid that sin from entering and contaminating your life. Then you must renounce that thing that overcame your father and overtook your mother! Renounce and openly disown that thing that compromised your grandfather and victimized the females in your family line. Forbid the approach of that alcoholism, fear, poverty, and sexual promiscuity.

Renounce the generational curse that lurks in the shadows and stalks your family members, infecting generation after generation of the best and brightest in your family history. Take up the authority that Jesus Christ won for you on the cross. Many people have been "converted" to a belief in Christ, but they have never taken the time (or understood their God-given mandate) to renounce evil. They have never taken the time to renounce wickedness.

RENOUNCE EVERYTHING THAT IS NOT LIKE GOD

The evidence for the power of renunciation is strong, and my convictions are even stronger. I believe the Bible is still right! If we share these convictions, then we know we must renounce everything that is not like God.

Renounce Everything That Is Not Like God

We must renounce every hidden tendency, every lustful urge, and every evil thing that tempts us from within and without. That's right! I must make a list. I must take time on my knees! It is time to renounce everything that is not like God, and embrace everything that is!

When you renounce and return, the very act of turning your back on the evils and failures of the past while turning your heart and face toward God *engages the ancient promises* made to the most storied band of rebels in human history:

But if from thence [the place of rebellion, presumption, failure, and sin] *thou shalt seek the Lord thy God, thou shalt find Him, if thou seek Him with all thy heart and with all thy soul. When thou art in tribulation, and all these things are come upon thee* [because you deserved them or brought them upon your own head through wrong choices and impure motives], *even in the latter days, if thou turn to the Lord thy God, and shalt be obedient unto His voice; (for the Lord thy God is a merciful God;) He will not forsake thee, neither destroy thee, nor forget the covenant of thy fathers which He sware unto them* (Deuteronomy 4:29-31).

By renouncing everything that is not like God, you free yourself to embrace everything, everyone, and everything that *is like* God. In fact, *it is your destiny!*

Now we have come full circle to the very passage where we began. The Scriptures declare:

Now the Lord is that Spirit: and where the Spirit of the Lord is, there is liberty. But we all, with open face beholding as in a glass the glory of the Lord, are changed into the same image from glory to glory, even as by the Spirit of the Lord. Therefore seeing we have this ministry, as we have received mercy, we faint not; But have renounced the hidden things of dishonesty, not walking in craftiness, nor handling the word of God deceitfully; but by manifestation of the truth commending ourselves to every man's conscience in the sight of God (2 Corinthians 3:17-4:2).

We've left deceit and deception behind with everything else that we have renounced and forbidden in our lives. Now we embrace the power of God to see, receive, and manifest or *demonstrate* the truth of God's love in our daily lives. Are you ready for a new beginning?

ENDNOTES

1. Victoria J. Barnett, "The Nazi Challenge to the German Protestant Church," gen. ed., *Dietrich Bonhoeffer Works*, English Edition, Director for Church Relations, U.S. Holocaust Museum. Accessed via http://www.bonhoeffer.com/bak1.htm on 7-19-07. She writes: "If they agreed with many of the political aims of the Nazi regime, many Protestant clergy and leaders nevertheless found the German Christian agenda to be ideologically tainted and anti-Christian. A new movement emerged, led by prominent preachers and theologians like Martin Niemoeller and Karl Barth, that opposed the German Christians: the Confessing Church...Although he was only 27 years of age when Hitler became Chancellor, Dietrich Bonhoeffer gained early prominence as one of the most radical voices in the Confessing Church...And in his writings he raised more universal questions...about the viability of religious faith in an ideological age

and the ethical demands of fighting against evil…Tragically, Bonhoeffer's prophetic voice was silenced only weeks before the Allied victory. Yet the German Protestant church that emerged from the ashes in 1945 was a very different one from the predominantly nationalistic church that had greeted Hitler in 1933. In the October 1945 Stuttgart Declaration of Guilt its leaders acknowledged their guilt and complicity in the Nazi reign of terror."

2. According to the article, "Dutch Reformed Churches," from the U.S. Library of Congress, "Christianity became a powerful influence in South Africa, often uniting large numbers of people in a common faith. In the twentieth century, however, several Christian churches actively promoted racial divisions through the political philosophy of apartheid. The largest of these denominations was the Dutch Reformed Church (Nederduitse Gereformeerde Kerk—NGK), which came to be known as the "official religion" of the National Party during the apartheid era. Its four main branches had more than 3 million members in 1,263 congregations in the 1990s." Accessed via Internet on 7/19/06 at http://countrystudies.us/south-africa/53.htm.

3. "Charges Facing Saddam Hussein," BBC NEWS, 7/1/2004: http://news.bbc.co.uk/go/pr/fr/-/2/hi/middle_east/3320293.stm.

4. Ibid.

5. *Strong's*, Greek #550, apeipomen, ap-i-pom'-ane; reflex. past of a comp. of G575 and G2036; to say off for oneself, i.e. disown:—renounce.

6. W.E. Vine, Old Testament edited by F.F. Bruce, *VINES Expository Dictionary of Old and New Testament Words*, Volume 3: Lo—Ser, (Old Tappan, NJ: Fleming H. Revell Company, 1981), p. 279, "renounce."

7. The apostle Paul revealed this principle as the method Jesus used to sanctify and cleanse the Church; and as the recommended tool for discipleship and encouragement in marriage relationships in Ephesians 5:24-27 (KJV): *"Therefore as the church is subject unto Christ, so let the wives be to their own husbands in every thing. Husbands, love your wives, even as Christ also loved the church, and gave Himself for it; that He might sanctify and cleanse it with the washing of water by the word, that He might present it to Himself a glorious church, not having spot, or wrinkle, or any such thing; but that it should be holy and without blemish."*

CHAPTER NOTES

Chapter 7

RESIST THE DEVIL AGGRESSIVELY!

FROM generation to generation since the birth of the art of storytelling, the human race has gathered to hear tales of heroes who dared to resist evil. The inner drive to hear the stories of triumph was just as strong around ancient campfires as it is to us today as we gather around state-of-the-art HDTV screens with enhanced theater-style sound systems or in massive auditoriums.

Many of the adults in any crowd of Americans will tell you they remember a school-yard bully everyone feared in childhood...and a few, just a few, will tell you the rest of the story. They'll tell you—and usually the telling comes with great delight—of the day the bully in their memory met his match and lost his mandate to rule the school-yard.

You and I face a bully that has brutalized the human race since the day Adam and Eve were ejected from paradise. The apostle Paul described his bullying role when he wrote, "*Wherein in time past ye walked according to the course of this world, according to the prince of the power of the air, the spirit that now worketh in the children of disobedience"* (Eph. 2:2). This prince is a brutal taskmaster and an ungrateful boss.

In 1965, at the height of the Civil Rights Movement and the nuclear tension of the Cold War, George Stevens produced a movie entitled, *The Greatest Story Ever Told.* The hero of the story was none other than Jesus Christ, who rose from the dead to defeat His foe and remove the bully's mandate to dominate our world. Blacks and whites alike gathered in darkened theaters to witness the story of hope in a seemingly hopeless era.

The Bully Still Stalks the Playground

Decades later, the bully still stalks the playground where he was humiliated nearly 2,000 years ago. He counts on our forgetting about his defeat at the cross and the tomb. He can only succeed *when we fail* to remind him—and others—of his defeat, failure, and absolute removal from power!

Perhaps it was for this reason that Peter the apostle warned us: *"Be of sober spirit, be on the alert. Your adversary, the devil, prowls around like a roaring lion, seeking someone to devour. But resist him, firm in your faith..."* (1 Peter 5:8-9 NASB).

James, the pastor of the first Christian church in existence, faced unbelievable opposition. He was pressured by Jewish religious leaders, prodded by people involved in internal squabbling, and persecuted by King (Herod) Agrippa. Agrippa ultimately ordered his execution by the sword 14 years after the

Lord's resurrection.[1] The apostle James became the first of the twelve "Disciples of the Lamb" to die a martyr's death. He was a man who was intimately acquainted with the bullying ways of the devil, but he defiantly declared in the face of it all:

> *Do ye think that the scripture saith in vain, The spirit that dwelleth in us lusteth to envy? But He giveth more grace. Wherefore He saith, God resisteth the proud, but giveth grace unto the humble. Submit yourselves therefore to God.* **Resist the devil, and he will flee from you.** *Draw nigh to God, and He will draw nigh to you. Cleanse your hands, ye sinners; and purify your hearts, ye double minded. Be afflicted, and mourn, and weep: let your laughter be turned to mourning, and your joy to heaviness. Humble yourselves in the sight of the Lord, and He shall lift you up* (James 4:5-10).

He Did Not Say, "Resist the Devil If It Is Convenient!"

Did you notice that highlighted verse from the letter of James the apostle? He told the early Christians, "*Resist* the devil, and he will flee from you." James did *not* say, "If it is convenient, then resist the devil." He did not say, "Resist until *it starts to hurt*, and then quit before you hurt yourself." And the apostle definitely did *not* say, "Resist *until it becomes unpopular* with your friends—I don't expect you to do anything politically incorrect." James did *not* say, "Take the easiest way to your goal."

You must resist the devil *aggressively*! James didn't say, "Play with him." He didn't whine, "Appease him." He didn't advise, "Hide from him." He didn't whisper in hushed tones, "Fear him." The apostle of God almost shouts to us from the pages of Holy Writ, "*Resist him!*"

Satan is not your friend; he's your adversary! The Bible says, "*Be sober, be vigilant; because your adversary the devil, as a roaring lion, walketh about, seeking whom he may devour*" (1 Pet. 5:8).

Would you allow your children or a young member of your family to play with a wild 1,500-pound lion? No! (Unless something is seriously wrong with you mentally.) Yet you essentially do the same thing every time you fail to drive the lion away from your home.

A law enforcement officer or soldier may possess all the delegated authority and firepower necessary to resist a violent offender or the driver of a speeding car. However, nothing happens until *somebody* steps in harm's way and blocks the path of the speeding car or challenges the violent intent of a mugger or armed robber.

Don't Play "Patty-Cake" With This Spiritual Predator

Satan hates you with an eternal hatred rooted in bitter jealousy! Don't cower from him and don't play "patty-cake" with this spiritual predator. You can't do that if all the devil sees is your "spiritual backside" as you flee from him! You must resist him aggressively!

"I hear you, but how do I do it? I'm just an ordinary Christian; what chance does somebody like me have in a shoving match with the devil?"

Begin where all spiritual truth begins—with God's Word. He said, "*Greater is He that is in you, than he that is in the world*" (1 John 4:4). He also said, "*Resist the devil, and he will flee from you*" (James 4:7).

You might think that the Church would have conquered the enemy and spread the Good News of Jesus Christ throughout the world by now. Unfortunately, *five problems plague the people of God and make us ineffective in our generation.*

Problem 1:
We don't recognize that we have an enemy.

Most Americans didn't realize that they had a mortal enemy—until the deadly attacks on the World Trade Center Towers, the Pentagon, and the jetliners on September 11, 2001. The truth is that al-Qaeda had been working overtime since the 1980s to attack American interests because of our support for the nation of Israel.

In February of 1993, a truck bomb exploded in a basement area under Tower One of the World Trade Center, killing six people and disrupting businesses for six months. Six Islamic militants were convicted in the bombing and sentenced to life in prison. Yet, at the time, no one (except certain groups in the defense and law enforcement communities) seemed to know or care about Osama bin Laden and a shadowy group called "al-Qaeda."

The American nation as a whole didn't recognize that it had an enemy, so we failed to prepare and defend ourselves properly. The same situation involving an unrecognized enemy led to the unprovoked but lethal surprise attack on Pearl Harbor, Hawaii, in

1941. That sneak attack *also* led to a declaration of war heard around the world.

Subterfuge, trickery, disguises, and false presentation as friendly, logical, and concerned "friends" nearly always figures into the mix of a secret enemy. Consider God's penetrating description of our archenemy: *"Satan himself is transformed into an angel of light. Therefore it is no great thing if his ministers also be transformed as the ministers of righteousness; whose end shall be according to their works"* (2 Corinthians 11:14b-15).

PROBLEM 2:
   WE ARE SUBJECT TO STRATEGIES AND ATTACKS THAT
   WE DON'T DISCERN.

The apostle Paul warned us in his Second Epistle to the Corinthians to quickly forgive others *"lest Satan should get an advantage of us: for we are not ignorant of his devices"* (2 Cor. 2:11). Now think for a moment: What if you are ignorant of his devices or schemes? The logical answer is also chilling: Satan gets an advantage over you! In modern terms, that means that satan has outsmarted you. He wins; you lose. And if he has his wicked way, you will lose *big.*

The truth is that most people—including a high percentage of Christians—seem to read the Bible as if it is a fairy tale. They pick and choose the "nuggets" they want to accept from God's Word like overstuffed children snubbing everything on God's buffet table except the sweet treats.

Many of us are more likely to quote our favorite newscaster, movie star, or comedian than we are to quote the Bible on any given day. Christians give up their "new-birth right" when they begin to apply the term "myth" to the Genesis account, to the existence of hell, and to the coming resurrection and judgment of the dead. From there, it is only a short leap to reduce the devil's existence to a mere myth, and the virgin birth and divinity of Christ to mere analogies and mental concepts. (As far as I know, no one has ever been forgiven of sin or redeemed by mere analogy or a mental concept!)

Think about this: *Your enemy* has had thousands of years to study human behavior. He has carefully perfected his collection of baits and hooks for the human soul. He knows every emotional and physical button to push, and he will do anything to subvert a human soul. He follows no rules and has no conscience.

Although you shouldn't fear him, you should certainly acknowledge his existence and learn everything you can about his tactics. That will help you prepare to meet and defeat his every attack with the Word of God by faith. The Scriptures make this simple but powerful promise to every true believer: "*Ye are of God, little children, and have overcome them: because greater is He that is in you, than he that is in the world*" (1 John 4:4).

PROBLEM 3:
    WE ARE SLEEPY-HEADED OR PASSIVE WHEN WE
    NEED TO BE ALERT AND AGGRESSIVE.

This problem helps explain why we wrestle with the first two problems of recognizing our enemy and understanding his schemes. *Why should we think ourselves exempt* from the spiritual forces that seduced early church members by lulling them into a spiritual slumber of compromise and gradual descent into sin?

The fact that we live in a modern age offers absolutely no protection. It may even make us more vulnerable to spiritual seduction because many of the Christians in modern societies are *tired*. Our extreme subservience to a careening, out-of-control, train wreck of a society is killing us. We have no time for anybody or anything except ourselves, and sometimes we even sacrifice *ourselves* on the altar of keeping pace in the rat race we call "life."

Paul the apostle used his pen to virtually "shout" this message through his letter to the slumbering saints of Ephesus:

Proving what is acceptable unto the Lord. And have no fellowship with the unfruitful works of darkness, but rather reprove them. For it is a shame even to speak of those things which are done of them in secret. But all things that are reproved are made manifest by the light: for whatsoever doth make manifest is light. Wherefore He saith, Awake thou that sleepest, and arise from the dead, and Christ shall give thee light. See then that ye walk circumspectly, not as fools, but as wise, Redeeming the time, because the days are evil. Wherefore be ye not unwise, but understanding what the will of the Lord is (Ephesians 5:10-17).

PROBLEM 4:

WE HAVE THE POWER AND DON'T REALIZE IT.

Then the eleven disciples went away into Galilee, into a mountain where Jesus had appointed them. And when they saw Him, they worshipped Him: but some doubted. And Jesus came and spake unto them, saying, "All power is given unto Me in heaven and in earth. Go ye therefore, and teach all nations, baptizing them in the name of the Father, and of the Son, and of the Holy Ghost: Teaching them to observe all things whatsoever I have commanded you: and, lo, I am with you always, even unto the end of the world. Amen" (Matthew 28:16-20).

Despite the three-and-a-half years the disciples had spent in the literal presence and under the direct teaching and ministry of Christ, those 11 men were still shocked when Jesus said, "All power has been given to Me." Some of them still *doubted.* Think about that: Here is Jesus, standing in front of them after having been crucified and resurrected, and they *still doubted?* (It sounds a lot like the modern Church.)

You would *think* those men would have known better. After all, they were there the day Jesus appointed 70 people from the group of followers and sent them out with authority. They were also there the day the 70 returned in amazement with stories of casting out devils and healing the sick (see Luke 10). Jesus redirected their amazement toward the mercy that God was showing them by adding their names to the Lamb's book of life, and He said something the Church has largely forgotten for the last 2,000 years! *"Behold, I give unto you power to tread on serpents and scorpions, and over all the power of the enemy: and nothing shall by any means hurt you*" (Luke 10:19).

Notice three things about this promise from Jesus: (1) He addressed it in front of *everyone present*, not merely to the Twelve Disciples; (2) He said, "I give unto *you*"; and (3) *what* He gave us was power over *all the power of the enemy*.

You don't have to be a Bible scholar to understand the importance and consequences of this statement. Was Jesus serious, or "just joking around"? Did He mean what He said, or was He just mouthing platitudes like so many Christians do today? The answers to these questions are obvious, but what *isn't so obvious* is why we don't operate in this power today!

PROBLEM 5:

WHEN WE DO REALIZE WE HAVE IT,
WE DON'T USE THE POWER GOD HAS GIVEN US!

Why would Jesus give you and I power unless He fully intended for us to use it? Was this authority just given to people for a temporary show? (Have we *ever* known God to do *anything* for a temporary show?)

What if you carried a vaccine, an amazing antidote, in your pocket and walked among hospital patients who were dying from the disease for which that antidote was made, yet you refused to say anything about the medicine or to distribute it among the fatally ill? Wouldn't you think you would be charged with criminal negligence?

Honestly, you *do* carry God's vaccine for terminal sin in the "pocket of your heart." And you know the vaccine works, too! When we fail to share our vaccine (the gospel of Christ) with the lost, when we fail to pray for the sick *where we find them* (not merely in our church services), when we don't go the extra mile to set other people free, then we are squandering the gift of God! You have the power—now use it!

IT IS TIME TO RESIST THE DEVIL— *AGGRESSIVELY*!

You, *personally*, have the God-given power and authority to *resist* the devil! Are you ready to start right now? Make this declaration with me right where you are at this moment:

I resist everything that is not like God! I make a defense against evil! I choose to stand and plead the blood of Jesus over my life and over my dreams! I come against everything that would hinder my marriage, hinder my family, or compromise my future! I am a child of God, and I will serve Him only!

ENDNOTES

1. William Steuart McBirnie, Ph.D., *The Search for the Twelve Apostles* (Wheaton, IL: Tyndale House Publishers, 1974), p. 104. See also Acts 12:2.

CHAPTER NOTES

Chapter 8

RENEW YOUR VOWS TO THE LORD

Blessed are they which do hunger and thirst after righteousness: for they shall be filled (Matthew 5:6).

WHAT can a man do after he has betrayed his best friend—more than once? What is left to say when your public brag has been replaced by a public failure to walk your bold talk? How do you face a mentor who invested years of training and personal instruction in you only to watch you publicly humiliate yourself (and your mentor) in countless ways?

You do what Peter did when he met Jesus at the lakeside after the resurrection. You renew your vows. This outspoken disciple's return from shame began the moment he plunged into the water to reach the Risen Christ as fast as he could. In one heart-gripping instant, all thoughts of shame, sorrow, regret, or loss were put aside with the possibility that once again Peter could look upon the face of the One he loved!

Peter is the man who would write toward the end of his earthly ministry, *"And above all things have fervent love for one another, for 'love will cover a multitude of sins'"* (1 Pet. 4:8 NKJV).

In his frantic rush to get back into the Lord's presence Peter couldn't wait for his fishing vessel to make the shore. Once again he left the security of the ship for the uncertainty of the water to go to his Master. And this time, only a matter of days after the soul-crushing failures and losses of the crucifixion, Peter would humbly renew his vows after a supernatural meal provided and prepared by Jesus. In this exchange between Jesus and His most outspoken follower, we see the eternal *truth* and real-life *reality* behind Peter's words—*love really does cover a multitude of sins!*

Three times Peter had publicly denied his Lord, and three times the Lord asked Peter if he loved Him. Each renewal of Peter's vow of love echoed specific events, boasts, and missteps from his life...and each time Peter's reply grew even humbler.

So when they had dined, Jesus saith to Simon Peter, "Simon, son of Jonas, lovest thou Me more than these?" He saith unto Him, "Yea, Lord; Thou knowest that I love Thee." He saith unto him, "Feed My lambs." He saith to him again the second time, "Simon, son of Jonas, lovest thou Me?" He saith unto Him, "Yea, Lord; Thou knowest that I love Thee." He saith unto him, "Feed My sheep." He saith unto him the third time, "Simon, son of Jonas, lovest thou Me?" Peter was grieved because He said unto him the third time, "Lovest thou Me?" And he said unto Him, "Lord, Thou knowest all things; Thou knowest that I love Thee." Jesus saith unto him, "Feed My sheep" (John 21:15-17).

Peter the denier repented of his failures, renewed his vows, and then finished his race with honor. Thirty-four years later, the apostle Peter followed His Savior's steps to the cross, and was crucified upside down as a faithful martyr for the Lord Jesus Christ.[1]

Another troubled disciple who had struggled with failure witnessed Peter's plunge into the water and his renewal of vows, and he understood what was going on. He knew the stinging pain of failure, and he also knew the healing power of his Lord's gentle rebuke. He will forever be remembered for something he quickly outgrew, but "doubting Thomas" *had already been led through a "renewal of faith"* by the Lord in a closed room only eight days after the resurrection. We don't know if Thomas was "wired" to think like a detective or a logician, but for whatever reason, he had demanded physical proof of God's spiritual reality. Jesus gave it to him but with a stern command.

Now Thomas, called the Twin, one of the twelve, was not with them when Jesus came. The other disciples therefore said to him, "We have seen the Lord." So he said to them, "Unless I see in His hands the print of the nails, and put my finger into the print of the nails, and put my hand into His side, I will not believe." And after eight days His disciples were again inside, and Thomas was with them. Jesus came, the doors being shut, and stood in the midst, and said, "Peace to you!" Then He said to Thomas, "Reach your finger here, and look at My hands; and reach your hand here, and put it into My side. Do not be unbelieving, but believing." And Thomas answered and said to

Him, "My Lord and my God!" Jesus said to him, "Thomas, because you have seen Me, you have believed. Blessed are those who have not seen and yet have believed" (John 20:24-29 NKJV).

"Doubting Thomas" embraced his divine correction and quickly learned the higher value of believing without seeing. Thomas became a foundation for the unborn generations of believers to come.

We know more about the ministry of Thomas than any of the other apostles (except John and Peter). According to solid historical sources and Church tradition, the apostle Thomas established churches throughout the Middle East and in India, winning thousands to the Lord before his martyrdom for Christ.[2]

Another man of that era did such incredible damage to good people in the name of religious zeal that his name inspired fear in multiple countries. He had been carefully groomed by his nation's religious and intellectual elite for a position of power and influence. But in one day his vision for that life was taken away, and his entire life's work was reduced to a trash heap in his own eyes. Saul of Tarsus would become Paul the apostle and write these words in a letter addressed to the believers at an Asian city named Corinth: *"For I am the least of the apostles, that am not meet to be called an apostle, because I persecuted the church of God. But by the grace of God I am what I am..."* (1 Corinthians 15:9-10).

At times, entire church bodies must renew their vows! We see this in our Lord's demand to the Church of Ephesus: *"Nevertheless I have somewhat this thee, because thou hast left thy first love. Remember therefore from whence thou art fallen, and repent, and do the first works; or else I will come unto thee quickly, and will remove thy candlestick out of his place, except thou repent*" (Rev. 2:4-5). Most of the seven churches addressed in the Revelation were warned to renew their vows and correct their ways.

Here is the Good News about renewal and restoration: if you *really want* to please God, then He will meet you where your strength and ability fail. (There isn't room for Him until you reach that point.) He will meet you there even if you've already failed many times. If that isn't true, then David has no place in the Bible.

Remember that King David, the person God called "a man after Mine own heart," *failed, often* and on numerous occasions. He failed as a husband. Although he already had two wives, David had an affair with another man's wife (see 2 Sam. 11:4). David failed as a law-abiding citizen when he premeditated and authorized the death of Bathsheba's husband to cover up his own adultery (see 2 Sam. 11:14-15). Israel's greatest king also failed miserably as a parent because he showed favoritism among his kids. He failed to correct his favorite sons, and it led to one son raping his daughter—leading to a brutal murder of revenge by David's "number one" son and crown prince, Absalom. Ultimately, Absalom worked his father's weakness until he could incite open rebellion against David's throne (see 2 Sam. 13–18).

God still used and kept His promises to David despite the man's many failures. Even more amazing to me is the fact that God still openly claimed David as His own in both the Old and the New Testaments (see 1 Sam. 13:14; Acts 13:22).

David was quick to repent from the heart, and God was quick to forgive. This should give hope to all of us who face the need to renew our vows unto the Lord after failure. This is not permission to sin like the devil and have church like a saint—nor is it an encouragement to "work hard" at righteousness. It is an all-out attempt to lead you to the feet of Jesus where all of His power is waiting to fill all of your weakness.

ABANDON THE SEARCH AT THE RELIGIOUS RAG PILE

The Bible says that our do-it-yourself righteousness is "*as filthy rags*" in Isaiah 64:6. Then perhaps God can't really enter our lives with divine help until we've exhausted our futile do-it-yourself soul improvement efforts at the religious rag pile.

Jesus came to announce a season of favor, promotion, and prosperity for the pure in heart, but He never said they were "perfect" people. I'm convinced that one of the most hope-building statements Jesus ever made during His earthly stay appears in Mark's Gospel:

> *And when the scribes and Pharisees saw Him eat with publicans and sinners, they said unto His disciples, How is it that He eateth and drinketh with the tax collectors and sinners? When Jesus heard it, He saith unto them, "They that are whole have no need of the physician, but they that are sick: I came not to call the righteous, but sinners to repentance"* (Mark 2:16-17).

If you have a desire to live right and experience righteousness, then *God will meet you* halfway. But *you* must put something on the table by faith—whether it is your reliance on your supposed "strengths" or simply the burden of your obvious weaknesses. Surrender releases the resources of the Great Physician to heal what is sick, damaged, or wounded in our lives.

Then there is the lesson of desperation we learn from Bartimaeus, the blind roadside beggar memorialized in three Gospels (see Luke 18:35-43; Mark 10:46-52; Matt. 20:29-34).

His Desperate Cry Drew the Great Shepherd to His Broken Life

This was "the loser and son of a loser" who shouted above the crowd to a holy man he could not see. The power of his desperate cry drew the Great Shepherd to his broken life in the same way a lost sheep's bleating would draw a natural shepherd to an actual lost sheep's location: "*So they told him that Jesus of Nazareth was passing by. And he cried out, saying, 'Jesus, Son of David, have mercy on me!' Then those who went before warned him that he should be quiet; but he cried out all the more, 'Son of David, have mercy on me!'*" (Luke 18:37-39 NKJV). The Bible accounts tell us that Jesus *stood still* and *commanded* that the people bring this lost one to Him (see Luke 18:40).

As in the real-life and miraculous story of Bartimaeus, it is *there* at the point where our desperation for change and the Lord's provision for change meet that *our faith ignites God's ability.* In that divine exchange, the power of God is released into our weakness to restore the broken, stolen, or missing parts of our lives!

FAITH IGNITES GOD'S ABILITY WHERE
HUMAN DESPERATION MEETS DIVINE PROVISION

Of all the characters on the New Testament canvas, aside from Jesus Himself, Paul the apostle appears to be the most qualified, eloquent, and intellectually matched to the task of leading the infant Church into its destiny. Yet, this seemingly self-made man was perhaps the quickest to admit his weakness and proclaim his utter dependence upon God.

But He [the Lord] said to me, "My grace is sufficient for you, for My [God's] power is made perfect in weakness." Therefore I will boast all the more gladly about my weaknesses, so that Christ's power may rest on me. That is why, for Christ's sake, I delight in weaknesses, in insults, in hardships, in persecutions, in difficulties. For when I am weak, then I am strong (2 Corinthians 12:9-10 NIV).

In stark contrast, self-reliance slams shut the door of God's provision by repulsing His presence and making His promises powerless in our lives. It is far better to honestly face your weaknesses, losses, sins, and failings. These only heighten God's mercy and grace extended to His creation.

For you see your calling, brethren, that not many wise according to the flesh, not many mighty, not many noble, are called. But God has chosen the foolish things of the world to put to shame the wise, and God has chosen the weak things of the world to put to shame the things which are mighty; and the base things of the world and the things which are despised God has chosen, and the things which are not, to bring to nothing the things that are, that no flesh should glory in His presence. But of Him you are in Christ Jesus, who became for us wisdom from God—and righteousness and sanctification and redemption—that, as it is written, "He who glories, let him glory in the Lord" (1 Corinthians 1:26-31 NKJV).

Self-reliance slams shut the door of God's provision by repulsing His presence and making His promises powerless in our lives. This is why David declared, *"My sacrifice [the sacrifice acceptable] to God is a broken spirit; a broken and a contrite heart [broken down with sorrow for sin and humbly and thoroughly penitent], such, O God, You will not despise"* (Ps. 51:17 AMP).

Most of us have a problem accepting or admitting that we have a "broken spirit" or a "broken and contrite heart." Those conditions are usually associated with a crash, a collapse of everything we consider normal. So we hide our imperfections and cling to our false perceptions—blocking God's rescue resources.

WE FACE
"A QUESTION OF WILL AND DESIRE"

What experience do you have in God that will hinder you from going forward in the right way this year? Oswald Chambers declared in his classic devotional, *My Utmost for His Highest*:

My determination is to be my utmost for God's highest, to get there is a question of my will and my desire. It is not a debate, nor is it a thing of reasoning, but it is a surrender of my will and absolute irrevocable surrender on that point, which means that money cannot buy my will, friends cannot buy my will, my will must be toward God....[3]

Our present enjoyment of God's grace is often checked by the memory of yesterday's sins and blunders. But God is the God of our yesterdays, and He allows the memory of them in order to turn the past into a ministry of spiritual culture for the future.

Chambers is saying that if the truth be told (no matter how we try to keep the news "quiet"), some of us "messed up" our lives last year. We blundered. We fell. We tripped up. We did not get up (and no one helped us).

"That doesn't matter," we mumble. "We didn't *want* anyone to help us."

The journey back begins with a glance backward and inward. It's time to take stock of the things we did (and didn't do) yesterday, and where we are going today.

If your car doesn't work, you evaluate it. Or you take it to someone who can evaluate it according to the manufacturer's specifications for proper functioning. When you trace down the problem, you know which path to take in the repair.

If your choices landed you on a highway leading in the wrong direction, the course correction begins with the knowledge of where you took the wrong turn or where the true destination lies. Then you can accurately plot a new course.

VEERING OFF COURSE WITH
YOUR EYES WIDE OPEN

Perhaps you are one of those who did *not* go the wrong way blindly. You veered off course with your eyes wide open. You messed up boldly. Perhaps you made the decision to turn your back on God, or you decided not to tithe. You decided it was more "advantageous" to lie to the IRS or to cheat on your spouse. Whatever the decision or series of wrong choices, you've come to the point where you can openly *admit* that it was your decision and your responsibility—*but you don't want to stay where you are.*

Oswald Chambers was also saying that even though you can't change what happened in your life last year or last month, your life isn't over. Allow God's mercy and grace to permeate your life. Freely confess your sins, failures, and faults to the One who already knows about them anyway. Repent of your wrong ways, decisions, and actions. Receive His forgiveness, and *renew your vows to the Lord.*

With God's help, you can transform your experiences in failure to say, "I will never get caught up in that mess again. I want to go forward in God, and now I will use my past failures as steppingstones of the Lord to step back into my destiny in Christ. But *this* time, it is through His help and strength and through no ability of my own."

Some of us have to witness a killing to experience the *practical reality* of a new birth. We renew our vows to the Lord over a casket containing our remains from yesterday.

Have You Killed Off
Your Old Man?

The Book of Romans tells you how to "kill off your old man" so that your new man in Christ can run things in your life. (Just in case you are a "skim reader" who likes to skip past Scriptures, understand that I'm *not* talking about killing off your father! Read on for details.)

> *Therefore we are buried with Him by baptism into death: that like as Christ was raised up from the dead by the glory of the Father, even so we also should walk in newness of life. For if we have been planted together in the likeness of His death, we shall be also in the likeness of His resurrection: Knowing this, that our old man is crucified with Him, that the body of sin might be destroyed, that henceforth we should not serve sin. For he that is dead is freed from sin. Now if we be dead with Christ, we believe that we shall also live with Him: Knowing that Christ being raised from the dead dieth no more; death hath no more dominion over Him. For in that He died, He died unto sin once: but in that He liveth, He liveth unto God. Likewise reckon ye also yourselves to be dead indeed unto sin, but alive unto God through Jesus Christ our Lord. Let not sin therefore reign in your mortal body, that ye should obey it in the lusts thereof. Neither yield ye your members as instruments of unrighteousness unto sin: but yield yourselves unto God, as those that are alive from the dead, and your members as instruments of righteousness unto God. For sin shall not have dominion over you: for ye are not under the law, but under grace*
> (Romans 6:4-14).

These verses aren't talking about "other people" at different times and in other places. They are talking about *you*, right *now*, and right *here* where you are!

I suppose that perfect people have no need to renew their vows, but then perfect people seemingly have no need of a Savior either. The rest of us, however, are in open and dire need of both! To *renew* vows means simply "to make new again." The Internet age gives us a nearly perfect picture of what it means to renew our vows. At times a computer seems to *disconnect* or lose touch with its host…the page on the screen stops responding, and the information seems to be frozen or stuck.

The solution is to press the *refresh* button. The Scriptures describe a divine *refresh* function that far predates any refresh function in the make-believe world of a digital computer network: "*Repent ye therefore, and be converted, that your sins may be blotted out, when the times of refreshing shall come from the presence of the Lord*" (Acts 3:19).

This is your answer when people ask you, "What has happened in your life that makes you so determined? What makes you so forceful, so faithful, so committed, so connected, and so consecrated?"

Once you describe your journey and process of renewing your vows, then you can declare, "*I will not be disqualified…* I may have disqualified myself last year, but I will not be disqualified this year!"

Endnotes

1.   Adam Clarke, commentary on John 21:19: "Ancient writers state that, about thirty-four years after this, Peter was crucified; and that he

deemed it so glorious a thing to die for Christ that he begged to be cru-cified with his head downwards, not considering himself worthy to die in the same posture in which his Lord did. So Eusebius, Prudentius, Chrysostom, and Augustin. See Calmet." (*Adam Clarke's Commentary*, Electronic Database. Copyright © 1996, 2003 by Biblesoft, Inc. All rights reserved.)

2.   William Steuart McBirnie, Ph.D., *The Search for the Twelve Apostles* (Wheaton, IL: Published by Pyramid Publications for Tyndale House Publishers, 1974), pp. 144-145. The author cites this specific historic quote: "…After establishing churches and ordaining clergy in the Middle East, St. Thomas came to this country [India] as deputed by his Lord. Here, too, he instructed thousands and thousands of people in the true faith of our Lord, baptised them in the name of the Father, Son and Holy Ghost, set up churches for their worship and ordained the necessary clergy to cater to their spiritual needs. Afterwards he endured various persecutions and consequently martyrdom for the belief and justice of our Lord, by a lance thrust by miscreants deputed by King Mizdi."

3.   Oswald Chambers, *My Utmost For His Highest*.

CHAPTER NOTES

Chapter 9

REHEARSE YOUR FUTURE

(AND BREAK THE POWER OF YESTERDAY'S SHAME)

Iwill not be disqualified because I choose to come into all that God has for me. I choose to declare and believe everything He says about me (and that includes everything God has for me, everything He has for the Church, and all He has for my family). Let me put it in plain terms: I want *everything* God has for me and those in my life. God gives His all and asks for our all. I want the full exchange, the "charter member package" of everything God's kids receive when they surrender to Him and seek first His kingdom!

Sometimes, the only way you can overcome a sorry past is to rehearse your supernatural future! It takes more than "hope-so, wish-it-were-true" emotional episodes of false faith to break the power of yesterday's shame. You must personally apply the blood of the Lamb, the power of the cross, and the authority of God's Word to yesterday's wounds. Only then can you receive today's remedy and activate tomorrow's promise! How can you rehearse your future if you never take the time to learn about your future in God's Word? The *only way* to get real-time confirmation from God's presence is through prayer.

It doesn't make sense that God's people would continue to suffer "for lack of knowledge," when all of God's wisdom and power in Christ awaits them in His Word and in their prayer closet! Let me help you: If you are doing that "one little verse a day" courtesy stop with God's Word, then *stop it!* That is the pattern and mark of an immature believer, of an immature leader, and even of an immature congregation! (Perhaps you know of an entire congregation that seemingly is taught to subsist on baby bottle portions of God's Word that have carefully been diluted down to the lowest common denominator of godliness and maturity!)

DO YOU "BINGE" ON SUNDAY AND
STRUGGLE MONDAY THROUGH SATURDAY?

If you "pray on the run" more than you *pray until He's done,* then you may resemble a "spiritual bulimic." This is one who binges on spiritual things on Sunday but seemingly purges all spiritual truth and struggles along on starvation rations Monday through Saturday! Jesus came to give you and I "*life, and that* [we] *may have it more abundantly*" (John 10:10 NKJV). He did not bring life *that is barely livable.*

The first modification needed to break the power of past shame in our lives is *a change of mind.* According to the apostle Paul, we "*have the mind of Christ*" (1 Cor. 2:16). But he carefully explains that this new mind doesn't step into the "driver's seat" (my term) unless we allow God to make room for it by *moving,* or displacing, our old ways of thinking.

But the natural man receiveth not the things of the Spirit of God: for they are foolishness unto him: neither can he know them, because they are spiritually discerned. But he that is spiritual judgeth all things, yet he himself is judged of no man. For who hath known the mind of the Lord, that he may instruct him? but we have the mind of Christ. And I, brethren, could not speak unto you as unto spiritual, but as unto carnal, even as unto babes in Christ. I have fed you with milk, and not with meat: for hitherto ye were not able to bear it, neither yet now are ye able. For ye are yet carnal: for whereas there is among you envying, and strife, and divisions, are ye not carnal, and walk as men? (1 Corinthians 2:14-3:3).

You Can't Receive New Things Until You Drop the Old Things

God's way of thinking doesn't come to you "naturally." It comes supernaturally through the Holy Spirit *as you do what God asks you to do* in His Word. You can't receive new things in your hands until you drop the old things you're clinging to so tightly. In the same way, you can't receive God's way of thinking until and unless you are willing to release your old thinking patterns.

This is so important to God that the apostle Paul described Jesus as *purifying His Bride—the Church*—through "the washing of the water of the Word." The context of this passage addresses the marriage relationship, but the spiritual application is unmistakable! "*...Christ also loved the church, and gave Himself for it; that He might sanctify and cleanse it with the washing of water by the word, that He might* *present it to Himself a glorious church, not having spot, or wrinkle, or any such thing; but that it should be holy and without blemish"* (Ephesians 5:25-27).

IT'S TIME TO GIVE THE BRIDE A
DIVINE MIND TRANSPLANT

So the only way Christ can prepare His Bride for the wedding is to give her (that's you and me) a "divine mind transplant," a supernatural change of mind and transformation of thinking. This is the *only* way we can be transformed from having "the mind of Mike" or "the mind of Lakeesha" to having "the mind of Christ."

Jesus described it another way to His disciples when He said, *"I am the true vine, and My Father is the husbandman. Every branch in Me that beareth not fruit He taketh away: and every branch that beareth fruit, He purgeth it, that it may bring forth more fruit. Now ye are clean through the word which I have spoken unto you"* (John 15:1-3).

According to Ephesians 1:3, we have *already* been given *"all spiritual blessings in heavenly places in Christ"*! When Paul went on to list some of the most important things provided by Christ Jesus, he specifically included these things having to do with our *thinking*:

In whom we have redemption through His blood, the forgiveness of sins, according to the riches of His grace; wherein He hath abounded toward us in all wisdom and prudence; having made known unto us the mystery of His will, according to His good pleasure which He hath purposed in Himself (Ephesians 1:7-9).

DISCOVER AND REHEARSE YOUR
NEW FAMILY IDENTITY

The blessings of God and His divine wisdom are already available and waiting for us. Now we must begin to discover and *rehearse* our new family identity, privileges, responsibilities, and vision. We don't come up with these things on our own; we get them:

1. from God's Word,

2. from His presence (as the Holy Spirit communes with us through prayer, praise and worship, and meditation), and

3. from His instructors (the men and women of God He puts in our lives).

Let me get practical—*really* practical—for a moment. If you are feeding your spirit just one verse from the Scriptures each day, then you are starving your spiritual man or woman. Work your way up to at least a chapter a day. The act of reading the Scriptures doesn't make you more holy, but when you "download" God's way of thinking into your mind and spirit, you are loading ammunition in your spiritual weapon. Wake up with praise from the Psalms, and go to bed with wisdom from the Book of Proverbs. You are packing eternal wisdom into your "spiritual computer" so that through your obedience, *God* will make you holy.

Feed your soul a noontime meal based on spiritual meat from the Gospels or the Epistles. Boost your spiritual faith level and enrich your diet with staples from the Old Testament books of history, the prophets, and the patriarchs. Carve out or reserve some time in the middle of the day. Then lift your hands in prayer and praise. Go into the bathroom, or go someplace on your lunch break where you can pray aloud:

Lord, I need You. I just want to remind You that I'm Your child, and I need You. I need You today. I need You this afternoon, and I'm going to need You tonight and tomorrow morning. I'll need You next month, and the next and the next after that!

I want God. In fact, I want everything God has for me—and I don't want anything to disqualify me along the way. King Saul disqualified himself through disobedience, even after he was given God's blessing, anointing, and appointment to lead. His choice to please people rather than please God was so distasteful to the Lord that He told Israel's first king through the prophet Samuel, *"Because thou hast rejected the word of the Lord, He hath also rejected thee from being king"* (1 Sam. 15:23).

In other words, God was saying to this man, "What makes you think that because you are the king, you won't be rejected?" That is a good question to ask one another today: "What makes you think that because you have a position of leadership or authority, that you are somehow exempt from obeying God?"

No One Has a "Special Privilege" or "Right" to Overrule the Scriptures

This challenge faces every one of us who has been given authority in God's earthly kingdom. Even as parents, if we don't watch it we may begin to feel as if our authority grants us "special privileges" and the "right" to slip past or overrule the specific commands and authority of God in the Scriptures.

"Well, I know that is what the Bible says, but as a leader, I sometimes have to 'bend' the Word in the interest of getting the job done and advancing the Kingdom a little quicker or more efficiently." (Saul couldn't have said it better if he tried…and he did.)

If you ever find yourself wondering why things are beginning to "dry up on the vine," then quickly conduct a do-it-yourself spiritual audit or examination. You'll be fine if the evidence indicates you are merely encountering a dry season while following hard after the Lord, or that persecution has come because of your obedience to God in the face of public opinion or political correctness.

HAS INFLATED THINKING BROUGHT TROUBLE TO YOUR HOUSE?

However, if trouble has come to your house because you've begun to think higher of yourself than you ought, then watch out. The writer of the Book of Romans warned us, *"For I say, through the grace given unto me, to every man that is among you, not to think of himself more highly than he ought to think; but to think soberly* [or with sound judgment], *according as God hath dealt to every man the measure of faith"* (Romans 12:3).

That means we must never have an exaggerated estimate of our own importance! Look deeply into the spiritual mirror of God's Word, and make sure your head hasn't become "puffed up" with self-importance, selfish pride, or foolish presumption.

Make sure you aren't candy-coating some secret sins in your life. Nothing gets by God. Nothing! That should be both troubling and comforting to you as a true believer—*troubling* because you know you'll be the one-in-a-hundred who gets caught because you are a King's kid—*comforting* because it is proof that your heavenly Father loves you enough to set loving boundaries for your safety. God is saying, "I am interested in more than nice church clothes, high-sounding titles, and carefully choreographed presentations of outward righteousness. I want your heart to be pure."

I want God to do a work inside me. I cry out with David the Psalmist, "*Search me, O God, and know my heart: try me, and know my thoughts: And see if there be any wicked way in me, and lead me in the way everlasting*" (Psalm 139:23-24).

That is also why Proverbs 19 makes such a pointed argument against lying and untruth:

> *Better is the poor that walketh in his integrity, than he that is perverse in his lips, and is a fool. Also, that the soul be without knowledge, it is not good; and he that hasteth with his feet sinneth. The foolishness of man perverteth his way: and his heart fretteth against the Lord. Wealth maketh many friends; but the poor is separated from his neighbour. A false witness shall not be unpunished, and he that speaketh lies shall not escape (Proverbs 19:1-5).*

It is a sad fact that many of us are gifted—unfortunately, we seem to demonstrate through our choices, actions, and words that we are gifted as *liars*.

"I don't ever lie."

Let me back you up against the wall and put your job on the line. If the truth might possibly lead to your firing, whereas a "slight untruth" could save your job or even lead to a promotion, what would you do? Would you throw yourself on God's mercy and tell the truth regardless of the consequences, or would you look away and "fudge a little" on the truth today before repenting tomorrow?

PEOPLE ARE
WATCHING YOU

Completely aside from the fact that lying is a sin, there is another reason you and I must not lie. No one lives in a vacuum. If you have children, or if you spend part of your week around coworkers or other people in any situation, then people *are watching you.* Lying is highly contagious. As the leader goes, so go the followers. As the parents go, so go the children. As the president goes, so goes the company or the nation. As the pastor goes, so goes the church congregation.

The children of liars tend to become even worse liars than their parents. Lying and deceptive parents have a difficult time correcting lying or deceptive children; just as smoking parents find it difficult or impossible to tell their children not to smoke. It doesn't work to say, "Do as I say, not as I do." Hypocrisy never plays well on young ears (or older ears for that matter).

It is important to teach our children (and anyone else who is watching) how to rehearse life as God decrees it rather than as other people misread it. If other folks see us deal with our failures by openly admitting them, giving them to God, and rehearsing our future accord to His Word, then they will have no doubt that God is at work in us!

We have to learn how to obey God and pattern our steps after His Word. If we can ever learn—and teach our children—that *God's Word protects us*, then things will go well with us. If God says don't hang around or go with evil associates or friends, then don't go anywhere with them and don't hang around with them. If His Word says, "Don't date her. Do not be unequally yoked with unbelievers," then don't date her. When God's Word says something like this that is unmistakably clear, don't assume it only applies to "that other guy" on the other end of the pew—the one you are convinced is worse than you are. *"Be ye not unequally yoked together with unbelievers: for what fellowship hath righteousness with unrighteousness? and what communion hath light with darkness?"* (2 Corinthians 6:14).

She's not for you. Don't date him; he's not for you. Don't take that job; it will constantly pressure you to compromise your faith and betray your conscience. Don't go into business with the man who scoffs at God or discounts His Word; you are courting disaster. Instead, begin to rehearse your future as God decrees it in His Word! Every open door is not from God, but every open door in God's Word is *for you!* Begin your rehearsal for a new life with this prayer to the Lord who has given you the abundant life:

Dear Father, Your word says that when we come to You and surrender all, then we become new creatures. You said, *"Old things are passed away, behold, all things...become new"* (2 Cor. 5:17). I really need a new beginning because I've failed in so many ways that I've lost count. But I come to You right now asking forgiveness for my many sins and failures. I'm calling upon Your name, Lord. I thank You for Your Word, which remains a lamp to my feet and a light to my pathway. Breathe Your divine breath into my life. I'm staking my future on Your Word, Lord.

You said in Matthew 6, verses 31 through 33:

"Therefore take no thought, saying, What shall we eat? or, What shall we drink? or, Wherewithal shall we be clothed? (For after all these things do the Gentiles seek:) for your heavenly Father knoweth that ye have need of all these things. But seek ye first the kingdom of God, and His righteousness; and all these things shall be added unto you."

I'm rehearsing Your Words concerning my future. I humble myself before Your mighty hand, and I lay down my burdens and weights at Your feet according to First Peter 5:6-7, knowing that You truly care for me. I trust You to lift me up and honor me in Your good time, knowing that You have promised to meet every need and to provide the faith and focus I need today for a fresh future tomorrow. I pray these things believing Your Word and standing on Your promises in Jesus' name. Amen.

CHAPTER NOTES

Chapter 10

LET GOD
REPOSITION YOU

EVERYTHING related to God-encounters with humanity involves *change*—radical, fundamental, total change in our nature, quality, and purpose for living. The very first encounter between God and man was really an encounter between the Creator and the created. According to the Scriptures, "*the Lord God formed man of the dust of the ground, and breathed into his nostrils the breath of life; and man became a living soul*" (Gen. 2:7). Everything was assembled and ready for action, but nothing happened until God breathed. It's still that way.

There are companies around the world devoted solely to collecting body parts for use as "recycled parts" in surgical procedures. Countless numbers of limbs, organs, joints, ligaments, muscles, and assorted body parts have been stored in a deep-frozen state for sale to the highest bidder. Yet, even a "complete" assortment of body parts does not a living body make. It takes a

God-encounter to impart life. The best we can do apart from the Divine Breath is attach recycled parts to a living human being— that is quite a feat, but it doesn't make us God-like.

In the same way, no assembly or assortment of ideas, "do-gooder" plans, experiences, or self-help schemes constitute a true "rebirth." Only God can fulfill the incredible promise given to us in His Word: *"Therefore if any man be in Christ, he is a new creature: old things are passed away; behold, all things are become new"* (2 Cor. 5:17).

God imparted to each of us (through Adam) the breath of life, but only He can take us through rebirth and entry into His Kingdom. And only God can *reposition* us beyond the reach of shame and give us a new name.

Headed for a Divine Repositioning That Would Change History

Consider the situation faced by a con-man son named "The Supplanter" (Jacob) who had become the black sheep of his biblical family through ethical failures and family betrayals. When this man heard that his angry older brother had assembled a gang to "gun him down," this guy sent his family members ahead of him as human shields and stayed behind out of harm's way. Jacob didn't know it, but he was about to have a God-encounter and a divine repositioning that would change human history.

And he rose up that night, and took his two wives, and his two womenservants, and his eleven sons, and passed over the ford Jabbok. And he took them, and sent them over the brook, and sent over that he had.

And Jacob was left alone; and there wrestled a man with him until the breaking of the day. And when He saw that He prevailed not against him, He touched the hollow of his thigh; and the hollow of Jacob's thigh was out of joint, as He wrestled with him. And He said, Let Me go, for the day breaketh. And he said, I will not let Thee go, except Thou bless me. And He said unto him, What is thy name? And he said, Jacob. And He said, Thy name shall be called no more Jacob, but Israel: for as a prince hast thou power with God and with men, and hast prevailed. And Jacob asked Him, and said, Tell me, I pray Thee, Thy name. And He said, Wherefore is it that thou dost ask after My name? And He blessed him there. And Jacob called the name of the place Peniel: for I have seen God face to face, and my life is preserved (Genesis 32:22-30).

THE MAKING OF A REAL MAN
THROUGH FACE-TO-FACE ENCOUNTER

The "man" whom Jacob wrestled that night was no mere man. We are peering through the divine window of destiny at the making of a real man. It occurred through a face-to-face encounter with the pre-incarnate Christ appearing in human form *before* His miraculous birth as a human being. What occurred in Genesis is that Jacob became a man after he wrestled with the Lord. In fact, the Lord still wrestles with men and women of destiny in order to wound their self-sufficiency, supernaturally reposition them, and give them a new name.

After Jacob's encounter with God at the creek, we find him *at the head* of the line awaiting the "angry elder brother" and his

400-man band of armed men. When God confronts you with your true destiny, something has to give! You will not emerge from that encounter the same as when you went into it. You will come out of that encounter transformed from child to adult, saying: "The Lord has changed my name, and I am a man"; or "The Lord has changed my name, and I am a woman."

Not knowing whatever else happened that night in Jacob's life, we do know from the Scriptures that he emerged with some backbone that wasn't there before the wrestling match! He also left that wrestling match with the favor and blessings of God. It turned out that Brother Esau greeted Jacob with a smile and a warm hug rather than anger. Jacob expected annihilation, but God gave him a joy-filled family reunion instead. Nothing can match the favor of God for miraculous turn-around power.

Many of us—or *most* of us who will openly admit that we've failed in life—may identify personally with Gideon, a man who is one of the Bible's "most reluctant heroes."

And there came an angel of the Lord, and sat under an oak which was in Ophrah, that pertained unto Joash the Abiezrite: and his son Gideon threshed wheat by the winepress, to hide it from the Midianites. And the angel of the Lord appeared unto him, and said unto him, The Lord is with thee, thou mighty man of valour. And Gideon said unto Him, Oh my Lord, if the Lord be with us, why then is all this befallen us? and where be all His miracles which our fathers told us of, saying, Did not the Lord bring us up from Egypt? but now the Lord hath forsaken us, and delivered us into the hands of the Midianites. And the Lord looked upon him, and said, Go in this thy might, and thou shalt save Israel from the hand of the

Midianites: have not I sent thee? And he said unto Him, Oh my Lord, wherewith shall I save Israel? Behold, my family is poor in Manasseh, and I am the least in my father's house. And the Lord said unto him, Surely I will be with thee, and thou shalt smite the Midianites as one man (Judges 6:11-16).

GOD CALLS IN SPITE OF
WEAKNESSES AND EXCUSES

The thing you need to know about Gideon is that *God called him in spite of his weaknesses and excuses.* When God called, Gideon tried to hang up. He did his best to convince God that He was making a big mistake (as if the Lord was ignorant of Gideon's many short-comings). This young coward (he was hiding from sight when God found him) went down the list, ticking off all of the high-lights of his low points. After all, Gideon *was* the youngest member of his family. And that family belonged to the least of the tribes—the tribe of Manasseh—and Gideon openly admitted that he was the least in his father's house.

It is interesting to note that the tribe of Manasseh was a "mixed breed" or interracial tribe? When Manasseh's father, Joseph (son of Jacob), was serving in Egypt, Pharaoh gave him a high-ranking position and also arranged his marriage to an Egyptian woman named Asenath (see Genesis 41:45). Joseph and Asenath had two sons, Manasseh and Ephraim. Thus, Manasseh was half-Hebrew and half-Egyptian. At that time, Gideon's clan was the least in this lowly tribe, and the man felt ashamed (per-haps about his mixed ethnic heritage). If you haven't already experienced it, you should know that shame can make you feel and act cowardly, passive, and unworthy!

Gideon felt shame, so he made excuses to hide his disbelief over God's pronouncement that he was a man of valor. I want you to notice that God called Gideon a man of valor long *before* he had done anything to qualify himself for that title! It seems that the bravest thing this man had done was to sneak out to the abandoned winepress with a bag of grain to secretly thresh grain out of sight from his enemies. In other words, this great hero and deliverer of Israel had done no exploits at all at the time of his divine call. This should give ordinary folks (that's *most* of us) some real hope!

GOD CALLED GIDEON WHILE
HE WAS ON THE JOB

You don't have to be on a retreat or deep in meditation somewhere on a cruise ship in the ocean to get a supernatural call from God. The Lord called Gideon while he was "on the job" threshing grain in the winepress.

His first words to the man were words of destiny and prophetic declaration! The Lord said, "The Lord is with you, mighty man of valor." God's words will *transform you* if you receive them!

Adam wasn't even alive until the breath of God entered him. And he didn't begin operating in his destiny of exercising dominion over the earth *until God spoke* it over him and he received it. The same was true of Abram the moon worshiper, Jacob the con man,

Moses the failed prince of Egypt, and Peter the uneducated commercial fisherman.

You're not called and anointed because you are so great and gifted today. It is because God sees into the future and *voices* the call on your life. If and when you receive the revelation of what you were born to become, then you begin to live it out with divine power.

The Lord's call isn't based on the virtues, accomplishments, or resources in your life right now; it is based on His plan for your life with a view to your victories tomorrow. God calls us to service based on who we are becoming, not on who we are now. *The Lord calls you with an eye focused on your future*, but He always calls and equips *today*.

That also means that you must stop the enemy when he tries to disqualify you from service today over your shame for things you did yesterday! Don't let the fallen angel, the "accuser of the brethren," fool you! (See Revelation 12:10.) And avoid the people who allow him to speak through their lips all the time. I'm talking about the people who seem so focused on *keeping* you feeling ashamed!

There *is* life after the divorce. If in your heart you know you did your best, repent of the divorce and take some time to fully forgive and fully heal. Then move on with your life.

You did make a mistake, if you fell into sin—even if you feel you were "stupid and ignorant" for committing adultery with that woman or ignored God's open warning to stay away from that man and lost your good name—truly repent, and start over in God's mercy and grace!

Now it's time to get your good name back. Step back into the race. Brush yourself off, take a fresh breath of God's grace, and come back to the destiny and calling God breathed over you long ago. If you know people who are hurting and have lost their way, then it is your job to point them in the right direction this time around.

God, in His great wisdom, took Gideon, His reluctant hero, from cowardice to heroism in *small steps*. After the initial encounter at Gideon's hiding place in the abandoned winepress, God managed to move Gideon to the top of a hill where the town idol worship center stood. Once there, Gideon stepped up to start the fight that would eventually lead to freedom for His nation.

GIDEON DESTROYED HIS FATHER'S IDOLS AND WON HIS RESPECT

It all began when Gideon destroyed the "altar to Baal" which belonged to his father (see Judg. 6:25). What happened next is one of the most powerful (and overlooked) transformations of a family relationship in the Scriptures.

And when the men of the city arose early in the morning, behold, the altar of Baal was cast down, and the grove was cut down that was by it, and the second bullock was offered upon the altar that was built. And they said one to another, "Who hath done this thing?" And when they inquired and asked, they said, "Gideon the son of Joash hath done this thing." Then the men of the city said unto Joash, "Bring out thy son, that he may die: because he hath cast down the altar of Baal, and because he hath cut down the grove that was by it."

And Joash said unto all that stood against him, "Will ye plead for Baal? Will ye save him? He that will plead for him, let him be put to death whilst it is yet morning: If he [Baal] be a god, let him plead for himself, because one hath cast down his altar." Therefore on that day he called him [Gideon] Jerubbaal, saying, "Let Baal plead against him, because he hath thrown down his altar" (Judges 6:28-32).

So what occurred in the sixth chapter of Judges? *Gideon's father actually changed his son's name—his "least, smallest, and most no-account son"—from Gideon to Jerubbaal.* Why? It was because Gideon had demonstrated the courage to tear down the town's false altars towards Baal. Gideon destroyed his father's idols and won his respect!

Gideon's obedience to God literally transformed his father from the town pawn and idol keeper (the man who willingly built whatever abomination the Israelite townspeople demanded) into a lion who boldly defied the lynch mob that had come to his front door to demand Gideon's head.

FROM THE WINEPRESS OF COWARDICE TO THE HILLTOP OF OBEDIENCE

Gideon's family destiny changed the day God *repositioned Gideon* from the winepress of cowardice to the hilltop of obedience, and it was God who was at work to bring it about, not Gideon himself.

Do you realize that God was at work in your life even before you were born? Of course the enemy was at work too—he did his best to send bad people, bad influences, sickness, and terrible circumstances your way. But think of all of the "close calls" in your life. Could it be that *it was God* who saved you from those near-fatal car crashes?

Was it divine mercy that intervened when you tried to sneak out and go to the party only to find that your perfectly good car just wouldn't start? Was an angel of the Lord standing in front of that car? Was it the angel that kept you off the street the night somebody emptied gun clips into every car and everyone on that city street where the party took place?

Just in case you're wondering: *that was God.*

IT'S GOD'S JOB TO SUPERNATURALLY REPOSITION YOU— IT'S YOUR JOB TO FOLLOW

The Lord is always faithful to do His part, but He always demands some action on our part. He repositions us supernaturally, but He also demands that we *follow* Him in some way that requires faith and obedience.

When Jesus entered Jerusalem on a Sabbath feast, He visited the Pool of Bethesda and spoke to a man who had been unable to walk for 38 years. (See John 5:1-13.) The Lord asked the man if he wanted to be healed, and He immediately heard the man's excuse. It seemed that an angel used to visit the pool and stir the water on occasion. Whoever stepped into the water first at that point would be healed, but this man told Jesus he "had no man" to help him into the water.

The man was missing the point, but Jesus overlooked the man's excuse and his spiritual blindness to go straight to the point of the man's need. *"Jesus saith unto him, 'Rise, take up thy bed, and walk.' And immediately the man was made whole, and took up his bed, and walked: and on the same day was the Sabbath"* (John 5:8-9).

Jesus told this man to *reposition* himself three ways:

1. He told him to change his *position* of elevation (rise).

2. His position of *habitation* changed. (His bed would no longer hold him; he would carry his bed from now on.)

3. His position of *identity* changed. (He was no longer an *afflicted man who could not walk*—he was a whole man who could walk and follow God.)

God will preserve you, protect you, and keep you from evil as you commit your way to Him. He will keep you clean and holy, even when you hit low moments and seemingly don't care anymore.

YOUR ENEMY WAITS PATIENTLY TO *RUIN* YOU!

That is why you must let God cleanse your mind. The enemy waits patiently (it must be the only "virtue" he has—he will wait to ruin you just as patiently as a lion waits to waste an antelope) for you to become so frustrated with the issues of life that you will listen to his whispered suggestion for you "not to care" anymore. The Psalmist—a man well-acquainted with hard days, dashed dreams, and the shame of moral failure—pronounced the cure when he declared: "*Why art thou cast down, O my soul? and why art thou disquieted within me? Hope thou in God: for I shall yet praise Him, who is the health of my countenance, and my God*" (Psalm 42:11).

Don't let worry over your job pull you into the pit! So you lost the job; hope thou in God! He can give you a better one. So your wife left you for another man; put your trust in God—a *virtuous wife* is a treasure, and all good gifts come from God (see Proverbs 31:10; James 1:17).

You lost all of your money and all you have left is a mountain of bills. So what? Have faith in God: He owns all of the silver and gold in the earth. He possesses the cattle on a thousand hills. (See Psalm 50:10 and Haggai 2:8.) You can get everything back and more. Put your trust in God, who gives you the very "*power to get wealth*" (Deuteronomy 8:18)!

Satan Will Play You Like the Fool You Have Become

Satan wants to get you so depressed and down that you don't even care. He loves to see you throw up your hands and say, "Listen, I don't care, I just need some relief. I'm going back to that woman in the red dress. I'm going back to the bar...at least I can escape the pain for a while there. I'm going back to the home boys—they're not much good, but I don't feel so beat up there."

Don't be fooled. Once *satan* repositions you where he can have you, then he will play you like the fool you have become. Mercy and grace are totally absent from his being and from his fallen kingdom.

When God changes your name, He changes your nature. When He changes your nature, He changes your destiny. Now remind yourself and your neighbor that your destiny has been changed! Begin to declare the truth over your life. Declare it over your future! God is not concerned about your yesterdays; He is concerned about your tomorrow. Trust me: Your tomorrow looks much better than your today. Follow these simple biblical steps to allow God to reposition you and give you a new name:

1. Pick up your bed and walk.

If you really want to experience a new life in Christ, then pick up your bed of yesterday's excuses and limitations. Stop whining—after all, it's annoying. "The reason I'm like this is because I didn't have a father." Or "My father was in jail, and my mother was alcoholic." Or "The reason I can't get a job is because I don't have a car...."

At this writing, there are multitudes who have been raised without two parents and with great obstacles. Step over every obstacle. That's just the way it is *at the moment*. We can't change the past, but we *do* have the power to change our minds and reshape our destinies today! Pick up your bed and walk—God has already provided everything we need to succeed. Now it's time to walk the talk.

2. Pray.

Real men and women of God *pray*. The Christian life is much more than the "dressin' up to go to the church meetin'" thing. I applaud regular church attendance, but you have to *know* the God of the church to get anything out of going to the church of God.

The Bible says, "*I desire therefore that the men pray everywhere, lifting up holy hands, without wrath and doubting*" (1 Tim. 2:8 NKJV). Real Christians pray every day. They pray in the morning, taking up their cross to follow Jesus, and putting on the armor of God for fearless living and power over the wiles of the devil.

I suggest that you start your day with prayer, perhaps modeled after this one:

Father, I commit my day to You. Cover me with Your blood, rebuke the devil, and Lord, protect my children, my wife (my husband), and Mother and Father. Cover my sisters and brothers and their families. Guide and direct me today. Keep me in the center of Your will. And thank You for another day in Your service. I confess that You are Lord over my life, Lord Jesus. My life isn't my own, for I've been bought with a price—be glorified in me, Lord. I ask this in the name of Jesus.

Then around lunchtime, as you pray grace your food, take time to add something extra for good measure:

Father, thank You for providing this meal for me, and as I bless this food, I ask that You bless my life so that I might be a righteous wit-

ness for You and Your Kingdom. Remember the hungry and the homeless, and those who have and those who don't have. Remember my family this day, I pray, in the name of Jesus.

In the evening, don't just drag your body into the bedroom and crawl into bed. Take the time to pray—*really* pray.

Father, thank You for keeping me in Your hands all day long. Thank You for keeping my mind in perfect peace. Thank You for ensuring that no hurt, harm, or danger came near my family. I am thankful that I am not in the emergency room or the morgue tonight, and I want to thank You for Your many blessings. Thank You for Your anointing and for the blood of Your only Begotten Son that has washed away my sins.

If you do that faithfully for just 21 days, it will become a habit. I *dare* you to pray regularly for 21 days straight. If you are married with a family (and you are really determined), then I challenge you to pray individually with your spouse and each of your children, and to also pray with them altogether as a family.

When you step back and consider the way the world has changed into a globe covered with violence, sin, and deadly conflict over the last 20 years, then you realize that you can't spend "too much" time in prayer with your loved ones! Prayer will help you bridle your tongue and avoid temptation! That is why Jesus included the words, "*deliver us from evil*" in His model prayer (Matthew 6:13; Luke 11:4).

Somebody tried to cut me off in traffic recently, and he flipped me a "one finger salute" as he rolled down his window and shouted the "N-word." Everything within my sanctified soul wanted to "lay hands suddenly" on this misled creature. I had to call on the Lord Jesus Christ, and His blood, and His mercy.

I happened to be wearing my Episcopal cross that day, so I rolled down the window as I pulled up right behind my new-found friend. Then I cheerfully waved my cross and mouthed, "God bless you." I admit my motives were just a little skewed—I wanted this person to be ashamed and embarrassed that he had talked like that to a man of God. I'm just glad I prayed that day, because everything in my natural man wanted to deal with the situation in a naturally evil way.

No one likes to be treated with disrespect or disdain, and our pride can lead us to do things we regret for a lifetime. Unfortunately, the enemy knows that and so do other people. I'll let you in on a secret: This fear of disrespect or of being ostracized was exactly what prompted many of us to smoke our first joint or drink our first glass of liquor. Many a young man has been misled by older relatives who should have known better. How many times have fathers, uncles, or grandfathers said, "A real man can hold his liquor, boy."

Countless times, misled parents, giving in to the spirit of the age, have said, "Now we know you are going to smoke anyway, so you might as well take your first drag in our house. If you're going to smoke, then smoke around the house." They make the same foolish mistake with alcohol and teen parties with drugs or alcohol.

And millions of mothers have believed the lies of government-funded organizations and have supplied their daughters with birth control saying, "Well, we know you're gonna do it anyway. Nobody can live without it, so at least you should have some protection."

Pray so you will stay firm.

3. Pursue God.

Run after Him with your heart, your mind, your soul, and your strength. (See Matthew 22:37 and Mark 12:30,33.)

4. Praise the Lord.

High praises to God and battle go hand in hand! (See Psalm 27:5-6 and Psalm 149:6.)

5. Press through life's issues.

Real believers and followers of Christ learn the art of *pressing on*. Every day is not going to be Sunday. Learn to press through life's issues and refuse to let life's issues press on *you*. Make your declaration by faith in Christ Jesus:

> *I will not be depressed; I will not let this problem take me down. I will survive, and I will thrive because God Himself will keep me in perfect peace! I will lift up mine eyes unto the hills from whence cometh my help. Yes, my help comes from the Lord.*

6. Partner with someone who wants you to succeed.

That is one way to verify who your real friends are. Do your friends really want you to succeed—even if that means you may do "better" than they have done, or if it means you receive more honor, apparent anointing, or a better promotion than they have received? Are they happy that you purchased the house? Are they thrilled that you were able to retire debt-free and travel the world? Are they happy that your children were able to graduate college?

Partner with people who have vision. The old saying goes, "Birds of a feather flock together." If your closest friends and advisers have no vision or direction, then they will do their best to keep you at their level—living with no vision or direction. Partner with people who have at least what you have or more. Associate with people who love and obey God, who work diligently to preserve and improve their marriages, raise godly children, and acquire wealth to give it away in Kingdom enterprises.

David and Jonathan were partners in conquest, and they were great friends. They represent the fulfillment and model of the "friend that sticks closer than a brother" described in Proverbs 18:24. This kind of friend is open, honest, transparent, and in heavy pursuit of his or her divine destiny.

7. Position yourself to be blessed.

Position yourself for success. Get ready to receive the answer to the apostle John's anointed prayer and declaration over your life: "*Beloved, I wish above all things that thou mayest prosper and be in health, even as thy soul prospereth*" (3 John 1:2).

Position yourself to receive the anointing and to go to the next level in God. Make sure you "follow the cloud by day and the fire by night" (see Exodus 40:38). Don't be afraid or reluctant to position yourself wherever the fire of God may be. Move beyond the crowd. Position yourself to be happily married, to be a faithful spouse and a godly parent. Trust God that your gift will make room for you, whether your gift is singing, preaching, banking, catering, cooking, or cleaning! Remember that Jacob positioned himself by saying, "I won't let You go until you bless me."

Gideon positioned himself by saying, "Lord, I'm the least." When God was done, Gideon finally came to a new conclusion that essentially said: "I'm going to obey God and be the man that God calls me to be."

Prepare to have all that God says you were supposed to have, and don't settle for one iota less. He gave you a vision, *now pursue it.* He gave you a dream, so go for it and stop wasting time! You must separate yourself from anything that steers you away from or hinders your pursuit of your God-given vision, direction, and purpose. Get ready for tomorrow *today.* Prepare yourself, for tomorrow is coming whether you are ready or not.

CHAPTER NOTES

ABOUT THE AUTHOR

Don't miss the latest nugget from the street-smart Bishop from New Jersey. University-trained and street-wise, Dr. Donald Hilliard, Jr., can speak eloquently before the Washington elite one moment, and in the next he can preach Heaven's themes in passionate power before urban audiences in New Jersey, New York City, or to international TV satellite audiences.

Bishop Hilliard's messages satisfy the trained mind and *ignite* the hearts of the downtrodden and heaven-bound alike! He is simply a humble man of God bearing God's *relevant* message for men and women in the post-modern era.

Bishop Hilliard is the recipient of the Distinguished Alumnus of the Year Award from Princeton Theological Seminary, Princeton, NJ (1995) and Eastern University, St. David's, PA (1997), The American Baptist Church, USA Evangelism Award (1996). He was inducted into the Martin Luther King, Jr., board of Preachers at Morehouse College, Atlanta, GA. (1995).

Dr. Hilliard earned a Bachelor of Arts degree from Eastern College (now Eastern University), St. Davids, Pennsylvania; The Master of Divinity degree from Princeton Theological Seminary, Princeton, NJ; and an earned Doctor of Ministry degree from the United Theological Seminary, Dayton, Ohio, as a Dr. Samuel D. Proctor Fellow.

An ardent cross-cultural bridge builder, Bishop Hilliard served as the Group Convener and Mentor of the Donald Hilliard Fellows Doctor of Ministry Program, and visiting professor of Church Renewal at Drew University School of Theology, Madison, NJ; visiting chapel preacher and lecturer at Wheaton College, Wheaton, IL; a former member of the Yale University Center for Faith and Culture National Working Group; and a member of the Oxford Round Table, Harris Manchester College, Oxford, England.

Bishop Hilliard currently serves *The African American Pulpit*, the leading academic periodical on black preaching, as an executive advisory board member; and is a current board member of *Gospel Today*, he is a trustee board member of The Samuel Dewitt Proctor Conference. As the senior pastor to Cathedral International, Bishop Donald Hilliard, Jr., serves 6,000 members in "One Church in Three Locations," including The Cathedral International in Perth Amboy, NJ, The Cathedral Assembly by the Shore in Asbury Park, and The Cathedral Assembly in the Fields in Plainfield, NJ.

Cited by the American Baptist Churches (USA) as a model for church growth, the Cathedral International functions as a multi-faceted relevant church in which fifty ministries are at work in three cities, with many members traveling from throughout the four-state region of New Jersey, New York, Pennsylvania, and Connecticut. Bishop Hilliard and Cathedral International reach millions of homes across the globe through Streamingfaith.com, radio, and formerly, the Word Network.

Other Books by Bishop Hilliard

In the Grip of His Mercy (HCI Books 2005)

Faith in the Face of Fear (Evergreen Press 2002)

Safe Harbor Begins at Home (Evergreen Press 2001)

Somebody Say Yes! (Evergreen Press 2000)

Stop the Funeral (Albury Publishing 2000) 5,500 units.

**For more information about
Donald Hilliard Ministries**
www.cathedralinternational.org
www.donaldhilliard.org

Additional copies of this book and other
book titles from DESTINY IMAGE are
available at your local bookstore.

Call toll-free: 1-800-722-6774.

Send a request for a catalog to:

Destiny Image₍ Publishers, Inc.
P.O. Box 310
Shippensburg, PA 17257-0310

*"Speaking to the Purposes of God for this
Generation and for the Generations to Come"*

**For a complete list of our titles,
visit us at www.destinyimage.com**